PATHWAY TO DISCOVERING YOUR PURPOSE IN LIFE

Book for Teenagers and Young Adults
(A must read for parents & adults)

Jim Nelson

DEDICATION

This book is dedicated to God Almighty, the giver of life, knowledge, understanding, and wisdom.
Secondly, I dedicate this book to teenagers and young people everywhere. Over the years it became clear that the majority of young people don't really know that there is a definite purpose for their life and existence. This book is written to help in their process to discovering their purpose so that they can be fulfilled in life.

Thirdly, I dedicate this book to parents, guardians, youth groups and organisations working with young people everywhere, reading this book will help them to focus and help the young people in their care and lead them to discover purpose in order to lead a fulfilled life.

CONTENTS

ACKNOWLEDGEMENT

I acknowledge my family – my wife Josephine Nelson, for her contribution, patience, and encouragement. Thanks to Pastor Dr Aremu and Mrs. Funmi Aremu, who took time out of their busy medical career to contribute by way of editing, and thanks to Mr. Mark and Kate Carroll Youth Pastors at Victory Christian Fellowship Ireland, for making time to contribute through editing. I thank Mrs. Morenike Arisekola for her networking connections and for helping to publicise the work we do with teenagers, youth, families and the communities at large within Ireland and overseas. Thanks to Dr. Samson Dabbas, Pastor of Grace Foundation Ministry, Minna, Nigeria, (Author: Pray until Something Happens), who proof read and wrote a foreward for the book. Thanks also to Dr. Taiwo Akhigbe, author (The Dilemma of HIV/AIDS) for taking time out of his busy medical career to point me in the right direction for publication. Thanks to Pastor Israel Ogidi of Sovereign Church Otukpo, Nigeria for his immense contribution by designing the book covers. Thanks to Pastor John and Joanna Ahern of All Nations Church, Dublin Ireland for making time out of their busy schedules to edit and foreward the book.

My gratitude goes to Pastor Brendan & Pastor Sheila Hade of Victory Christian Fellowship, Ireland, for being my pastors over the years, for giving me the opportunity to study and graduate at the Victory Bible School, for creating the conducive atmosphere in Victory where I work with teenagers, youth and adults alike and develop my people's skills and experience.

FOREWARD

In his book Pathway to discovering Your Purpose in Life, Jim Nelson clearly outlines the steps that a young person should take in order to ensure success and fulfilment in their life. Through Biblical examples and practical illustrations, he helps the teen/young adult realise that purpose can be found if you truly search for it. He identifies the importance of the parental relationship with the teen/young adult, highlighting that if this is strong, the discovery of purpose will be inevitable. His encouragement of the young person to be an honest, open communicator is also very apparent and necessary. This book is a wonderful source of wisdom and insight for any person who is on the journey to self discovery. Highly recommendable.

Pastors John & Joanna Ahern
All Nations Church
Dublin, Ireland

I am excited to have personally read through this book. This is not an ordinary book, but an inspirational book motivated by God in the heart of the author to address issues that relate to teenagers and young adults. The author of this book is someone God has highly graced with the very deep revelation on teenagers and young adult, to impart the world with proven principles which he teaches.

The author of this book is a man of humility and his passion for the kingdom of God is amazing. I have read books on teenagers and young adult, but this one is of a different class. All the words contained in this book are practical and easy to understand.

It is with a deep sense of responsibility that I say the author of this book Jim Nelson is a teacher, mentor, and leader to this generation. This book in your hand will help you discover your God-given potential and help you maximize destiny in a hurry.

This book will change your mind-sets and put you at the top because that is where you belong.

I, therefore, recommend this book to schools, churches, teenagers, young adults, parents, pastors and youth leaders.

Dr. Samson Dabbas.
(Author: Pray until Something Happens)

Prayer: I pray for understanding of my purpose as I read in Jesus name. Amen

PREFACE

TEENAGERS, YOUNG ADULTS AND PURPOSE.

I am part of a team working with teenager and young people in social settings, churches and communities. For most teenagers and young adults, discovering their Life Purpose is a daunting painstaking challenge that never ends but, this book gives you a pathway to discover your individual life purpose for your total wellbeing, ultimate peace of mind and fulfillment in life.

Considering the purpose of this book, I believe the Lord is about to start a revolution in which teenagers and young people everywhere will start knowing and understanding that God had a purpose for their individual lives, and how they can discover it and walk toward living a fulfilled life within their family setting and outside their comfort zone in life.

It is important to know that God created you with a purpose in mind and it will give you joy to discover that purpose and live it out in this life.

INTRODUCTION

The burning desire within my heart is to help teenagers and young adults find their Individual unique Life's Purpose, to build their self-confidence, to discover their hidden strength within, to maximize their potential and experience fulfillment in life. This is what motivates my desire and zealousness to always want to work with the different age groups everywhere I go.

Through the vehicle of training, teaching, coaching, mentoring and public speaking sessions I am able to facilitate these events with the teenagers and young adult groups and individuals in an on-going basis. Young peoples' quest for self-discovery can be a daunting and costly adventure at the different phases of life's encounters. Therefore this book will help to minimize risks and dangers associated with reckless youthful adventures and also provide a safety net for young people, adults, families and the society at large.

The random questions that young people have in their mind and the lack of satisfactory answers keep them aspiring to more adventures. Consequently they get even more daring to find out things by a *trial and error* approach that is of no benefit to their overall health, safety, and welfare. This book provides a pointer to the benefit of teenagers and young adults alike

This book addresses teenagers and young people in general, however, it is a must-read for all age groups of people as it will help create opportunities for discussion, chat and create a rapport for an awesome relationship building between parents and young people.

Chapter **1**

Purpose

What is it?

According to Collins Dictionary, Accessed 08/09/2018, https://www.collinsdictionary.com/dictionary/english/purpos e, Purpose is simply defined by dictionary .com as *"the reason for which something exists or is made"*. Or it can be said to be the reason why you were created to exist in this world.

Water was created for a purpose. According to, everyday health *" It is known that our human body weight is approximately 60 percent water. The human body uses water in all its cells, organs, and tissues to help regulate its temperature and maintain other bodily functions."*.

Tree-People.org states that "Trees have a primary purpose for existence to combat climate change, when excess carbon dioxide (CO_2) is building up in our atmosphere, contributing to climate change, the trees absorb CO_2, removing and storing the carbon while releasing oxygen back into the air".

Water has a purpose, the tree has a purpose and similarly, other creatures have their particular individual purpose! The question now is: As for YOU, WHAT IS YOUR PURPOSE IN LIFE? *This is a big question that the younger generations of today may not be able to answer by themselves hence this book is written to help in discovering life purpose.*

When we carefully look at every creature we find the purpose in them individually and the purpose we discover of them present a 'solution' to life problems. Therefore, it is safe to say that your individual life purpose when discovered will in like manner present a 'solution' to life problems for the benefit of mankind. That means you are a solution to this world. All we need to do now is to find your purpose and we will help you through the process. It can be done and it will be done. By the end of reading this book, you would without any doubt discover the real reason why you exist in this world.

The only reason people fail in life is majorly due to their undiscovered or broken purpose.

Vagueness of Purpose

From my practical experience of working with teenagers/youths over many years in educating, training, leading, mentoring, coaching and motivating them to achieve desired results in what they do, they appear to present unparalleled degree of vagueness to life purpose, to no fault of their own.

For the young person unanswered questions, feeling lost within the crowd, not being sure of what is actually wrong or right, being told what to do all the time, not being heard but shut abruptly, not being able to have an opinion and the systemic oppression of teenagers and young people push them into debilitating frustration, *anger, and nihilistic* reaction to the life issues that they face daily at home, school, office and in the community at large.

According to webmd.com, *"By age 15, most teenagers are developing the ability to think abstractly, deal with several concepts at the same time, and imagine the future consequences of their actions. This type of thinking in a logical sequence continues to develop into adulthood".*

The above psychology theory referred, therefore, implies that as a teenager and as youths they are capable of engaging in logical discussions with adults and can make reasonable contributions if given the chance, especially in matters of interest that relate to their own lives and interests. As a young person, you should appear to be responsible and engage with your parents or adults around you to give them the opportunity to help you regarding *discovering your individual purpose in life.*

As a result of the presented vagueness of purpose during youthful development in life, large numbers of young people feel frustrated, and angry sometimes for not being sure about a number of things about life. A good number of young people react negatively to parents, adults and sometimes rebel in their own rights when they don't know any other way to react to situations. At one extreme, some young people get so frustrated and drop out of school not knowing what is wrong with them, others drift towards crime or criminal gangs looking for a support system that they can fall back to for support in their confused state of mind about life and purpose. Unfortunately, some to their own detriment end up on the wrong side of the road of life.

That is why today, we have an innumerable *undiscovered purpose* and hidden potentials wasting away when the world really need those purpose to fix its on-going problems. Now, it suffices to say, we know that every individual purpose is a solution to life problems; therefore it is our responsibility to help in discovering all the individual purpose out there, in every teenager and young people.

What do I see about my Life?

Teenagers / Youth Development

For the young person there is prospect for purpose discovery, Building Self-confidence and living a fulfilled life.

Being a teenager you face growing up challenges and you do deserve to be given the chance to express yourself. You need to not only express yourselves but also speak up so that your parent can render some help and point you in the right direction of Purpose.

Noticeably, great numbers of young people, (teenagers/youth) present a shadow of themselves, some present a split image of self, some others ask who am I and what should I be doing with my life? Some of these presentations are non-verbal so, for the parents to be able to render a support and be sensitive to the needs of the teenager, the teenager has to be sincere and honest by the way they present themselves.

As a teenager or young person, if you are not clear as to *what is* right and *what is not* right about your behavior, the right thing to do is to position yourself in such a way that *the adult can find an opportunity to take note of your involuntary behaviour, and be able to help. Tell your parent what you are feeling and how you see things. Open communication with your parent will do a lot more good than you not saying anything when you face challenges. Open up and speak up to your parent or to the well-meaning adult that can help.*

As a teenager, if you do not have a good positioning that may enable your parents to understand you and find a way to help you in good time, if the challenges you face remain prolonged in your life, they sometimes can turn you into an embittered, nihilistic teenager. That is why some young people become violent and haughty with uncontrolled aggression which some professionals of today call challenging *behavior; others may call it antisocial behavior.* These presentations that are prevalent in lots of young people today are due to no clear communication between teenagers and the parents.

For teenagers and young adults, the state of vagueness of the mind that lots of young people carry could be described as a dilemma *(a problem that seems difficult to escape from),* but if the young person gives parents and professionals the chance to focus and pay attention, then parent and or professionals can help the future generations discover their individual purpose in life and help them to live to fulfill it, whatever the purpose may be.

Young people, in general, need to understand that if parents and well-meaning adults are not given the chance to be of help, they won't be able to help in any way toward the young person discovering **purpose.** Furthermore, in a situation where a parent or guardian is not available there is one sure help, the Holy Spirit who is called the Helper. Therefore, whatever your position, whether your parent is around to guide you or even in a situation where your parent or guardian is not available to guide you as a young person, the Holy Spirit, the helper will provide you all the help you need if you allow Him. At this point you need to ask yourself, do you have the Holy Spirit in your heart? If you don't have Him, He can't help you. So, decide to welcome Him into your heart. It's your decision.

If you don't allow your parent to help, if your guardian is not available to help, and if you don't allow the Holy Spirit to help you, your struggle with yourself may spiral out of your control and force you to start doing things you never imagined, and instead of you being a solution to (your)society, you find yourself turning into a problem to yourself, to your family and (the) society at large. That is what we see in most societies of the world we live in today. As a young person you are not meant to be a societal problem, you were created with unique purpose individually, to be a solution to our world.

Suggestion: As a young person capable of expressing yourself, it seems the time has now come for you to start taking the initiative to open up to your parent, ask questions about issues that are vague, that are not clear to you and enter into discussion on matters that are of interest to you. This would present an opportunity for your parent to start knowing you more and be in a position to offer more rewarding support to help you discover and achieve your **purpose** in life.

Questions to ask myself as a teenager or youth to see where I stand:

1. Do I have any communication link between me and my parent/guardian/other adults who work with me?
2. Do I trust my parent at home or the adults at school or workplace?
3. Am I comfortable with myself to be able to speak to my parent or the adult who can help me?

*Note: it is understood that building relationship requires time (which may vary from one person to another). It is only after a relationship is established that **trust** is built, whereby you may become more comfortable to discuss yourself or your challenges with parents or an adult who you may perceive to care and is willing to listen to you and help.*

If your **answer** to the above three questions is not '**YES**', then, you can start by taking the initiative to speak to your parents or an adult who you perceive can be of help to you. and *say for example*: 'Dad, Mum, may I please talk to you for few minutes? It is something personal. This kind of request may surprise the adult especially if this is not the norm for you and the adult. But, that would be a step in right direction.

A Scenario: A young boy once thought he wasn't sure what his parents thought of him so he took the initial step to start asking questions and talking to the parents. He eventually got an opportunity and asked to see his father for a few moments. It was his first time to converse deeply with his Father. The question he had for the father was, are you happy with the way my life is going? To the amazement of the young boy following his question, the father's answer was, "I never thought about you in that sense". The father further said I go to work, you go to school, I provide food in the house and you eat and never go hungry. But from your question said his father, I probably have to pay closer attention so I can start observing you. Then he asked him the first ever question that got both of them talking: The father asked "who is your best friend and do you have any dreams for your future?" The young boy answered:" I had always thought you are my best friend Dad, but you are too busy and never get to spend time with me, as for dreams, the young boy said, "I would love you to teach me how to dream Father."

Note: *Conversation is unfolding because the young boy took the initiative even when there was no established relationship at the time of his first ever question to his father. It may not be easy but you can take the lead to start a revolution for your own good between you and your parents/guardians or other adults in your life. Discovering your Purpose in life is crucial, it requires teamwork between you and your parents, family and any professional adult involved in your life. Open up, give up shyness and speak, ask the first question, chat with your Father, Mother or the professional in your life who is willing to listen to you.*

The teenage boy David (who later became King David) , asked the adults around him a question, time and time again. He did not give up questioning until some adult responded telling him about a reward that awaits anyone who would fight and defeat a mighty skillful war giant called Goliath the Philistine. David asking a question is what opened the door to an adult who gave him a bigger answer than he was hoping for.

In Luke 1:34 Mary asked a question: How will this be," Mary asked the angel, "since I am a virgin?" That question opened the door to an answer that brought her peace of mind and a calm in her spirit. As a teenager or youth, dare to ask questions so that your parents or adults around you may start to know you and establish a good relationship with you as you grow and develop into an adult.

Zero In

Prepare your Heart!

Perseverance: means persistence in doing something despite difficulty or delay in achieving success.

Luke 8:15 "But the seed in the good soil, these are the ones who have heard the word in an honest and good heart, and hold it fast, and bear fruit with perseverance

Zero in

Matthew 18: 3
And he said: "Truly I tell you, unless you change and become like little children, you will never enter the kingdom of heaven.

Important note for the reader to digest: From experience in dealing with people (both the young and the old), people of all ages have their heads and minds filled up with all kinds of information which most of the times serve as a deterrent to learning something new and beneficial. Therefore, the reader is hereby advised to ZERO IN (to direct all of one's attention to someone or something). Meaning literally, put aside for a moment, everything you have loaded up in your head or mind prior to this, as we hereby prepare our hearts and minds to learn on the pathway to discover our individual life purposes. ZERO IN. Come with an open mind like a little child, focus and learn. The matter of discovering your Purpose in Life is a serious matter and must be treated with absolute focus and determination from you. *FOCUS.*

Many Facets of Life

God's Purpose for you is Specific, Measurable, Achievable, Realistic Within your Life-Time

John 1: 12.... To all who receive him .... He gave power.

This is one of the most amazing things about GOD. No matter what shape your life seems to be in right now, no matter what opinion people may have about you, it does not matter. If only, you can decide to make a choice to 'Zero In' today, ask the questions in your mind and receive the Word of God, HIS word has the power to transform and translate you into a brand new person in just a matter of time. *Your transformation will silence your critics.*

As a young person you may have been called all sorts of names, especially (the) bad and (the) ugly names, but if you can decide today and allow the Holy Spirit of God to step into your heart, you will be transformed before you finish reading this book and find yourself discovering your destiny in Life.

In Jeremiah 1:5 it says "Before I formed you in the womb I knew you, before you were born I set you apart; I appointed you as a prophet to the nations." As a young person you need to know that God knows you by your name, God understand what is going on with you and He loves you so much that He wants to prove His Love for you, to YOU, and the biggest way God does that is to show you the Purpose He has for you in life.

When I meet young people and in the course of writing this book for the youth, I often reflect on my teenage and youthful years when I was adventuring, exploring, making uninformed decisions that were to my own disadvantage and misfortune. Looking at my life then, I don't think I was much different from the young people of this generation, but now, looking at myself from the perspective of this book, I can say that whatever side of life you come from, your life can turn around if you discover your purpose, walk in it and be fulfilled.

In line with purpose I now write, teach, train, mentor and get invitations to places to show Gods' love to young people, by helping them discover their personal purpose in life. What happened that changed my life was me accepting the Holy Spirit into my heart and He led me into my Purpose which I am now sharing with you in this book.

GOD created you with a 'Purpose' and by His grace and with the help of parents and the Holy Spirit, you can find your Purpose through the process of reading this book.

God created you with a specific assignment in His mind, the *specific purpose* is always a solution to a problem in our world. So, you are a solution to this world and to mankind. You may feel like your life is up-side-down, however, you have a given purpose. All you need to do now is to discover your purpose so that you can get into the process of actualising it while you have your whole life in front of you to live out your Purpose.

Pause for a moment! and Say the following to yourself.

- *My life has a Purpose! There is a reason why I exist.*
- *My Purpose is a solution to this world and that means I am a solution to a problem in this world.*
- *Oh, My God! AM I A SOLUTION TO THIS WORLD?.*
- *God help me discover my Purpose.*

Self Discovery

All teenagers and every young person need to know that no matter what ! YOU are the object of God's LOVE. Accept it and believe it, no matter what you've done, what you think or how you feel, and it does not matter what other people say or think about you either. God loves you. Psalm 136:26 Give thanks to the God of heaven. His love endures forever.

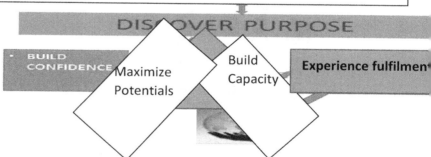

DISCOVER PURPOSE

BUILD CONFIDENCE   Maximize Potentials   Build Capacity   **Experience fulfilment**

A teenager once said, and I quote, "I don't know what is wrong with me", that was a statement from a teenager who was battling with the vagueness of self and without knowledge of purpose. However, with the help and support of parents and well-meaning adults, after you have overcome vagueness to discover yourself and your purpose in life, you can then begin to focus on building up your self-confidence, maximize your potentials by developing capacity, with an absolute focus on your life Purpose. When that happens, life's fulfillment will appear to be in sight in a way that *everyone around you will begin to notice the solution that you can be to this world through your **Purpose**.*

It's only after you have discovered your purpose in life that you can begin your assignment. Your purpose is your assignment. Just as you cannot solve a math problem without knowing the formula, in the same way, you can't be a solution unless you know the problem you are meant to solve in this life. Knowing your purpose is crucial and with the help of parents, well meaning adults such as teachers, support workers and most of all the Holy Spirit, your purpose can be discovered so that you can begin to live it.

TEAMWORK TOWARDS A WIN-WIN PURPOSE DISCOVERY

To teenagers and all young people: I wish to say that when it comes to discovering your purpose in life, it is an amazing journey that you can't take all alone. We know that parents, guardians, Pastors, youth workers, teachers, lecturers and other professionals who work with young people don't often have it all together themselves, but they often form the various teams of people who do help in various ways toward finding your precious purpose. Don't stand alone, there is the saying that, "*a tree standing on its own cannot make a forest*". Team up with your parents, families, and other loving and caring people around you who would give you the required support throughout the process of discovering your life Purpose.

On reading and digesting the information in this book. You will discover it's all about you and your purpose first. The journey to discover your purpose in life can be challenging, therefore, be advised that you need to cooperate with those around you who can help, such as your Father, Mother, Professionals and other well-meaning adults who care about your interest in life. Also, *you can arrange face – face training on 'purpose discovery' through your ministry, groups of people in your community and in your organisation.*

Going To the right places

Where do you go to spend time?

Who are your friends?

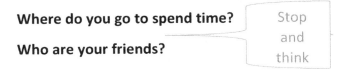

Stop and think

LET'S TAKE EXAMPLE FROM THE BEST WE CAN FIND!

Jesus is our best example because all over the world, even the world's religious founders and leaders do recognize Jesus as one in a class all by himself (actually, lots of religious books have the name of Jesus written in their manuals and positively talk about Him).   He was the first to introduce women liberation and gender equality during the time when, if any woman was caught in the act of adultery she was stoned to death but, the man involved with her in the act did not appear to be in the picture of the punishment. When a woman caught in the act of adultery was dragged and pulled aggressively to where Jesus was, He said to the accusers, "Let him who does not have sin cast the first stone" but, one by one every one of them dropped their stones and left the woman untouched. In the area of gender equality Jesus was the one who first introduced women ministers whom he allowed to do ministry (to Him), alongside his twelve disciples, such as Mary who anointed Jesus feet with an expensive alabaster oil: John 12:3. In those days, the act of anointing a person or a sacred object with an anointing oil was a ministerial or priestly duty (duty usually performed by male), but Jesus started a revolution by allowing female to perform same role, during the period when women were subjected to housekeeping duties as their confinement. Furthermore, Jesus was the first to introduce social unity in the episode when he met the woman at the well in Samaria and asked her for a drink of water. Whereas, at the time the societal disunity and disagreement dis not permit a Jew to ask of such a favour from Samaritans

The above few instances suffice for us to use Jesus as our best available enviable example in our quest to discover our individual unique purpose in life. Jesus discovered his Purpose was to be the mediator between the creator and his creation. **Luke 4:16-18**: [16] He went to Nazareth, where he had been brought up, and on the Sabbath day he went into the synagogue, as was his custom. He stood up to read, [17] and the scroll of the prophet Isaiah was handed to him. Unrolling it, *he found the place* where it is written: [18] "The Spirit of the Lord is on me, because he has anointed me
   to proclaim good news to the poor. He has sent me to proclaim freedom for the prisoners
   and recovery of sight for the blind,
to set the oppressed free,... (*His example points out for us to take steps in the right direction, go to the right places, get the help we need and discover our destiny to fulfil it). The story also reveals that Jesus was helped by his earthly parents, at the synagogue someone helped pass on the scroll to him, and in the process of him doing the right thing by reading the right book, he discovered his destiny and thereafter lived life to fulfil it.*

Chapter **2**

Purpose as a Hidden Treasure

Pupose is a hiden treasure that the young person will need the cooperation of the parent to discover, therefore it is vital that the parent create the right environment and atmosphere to work together with the young person. *Ephesians 6:4* Fathers, do not provoke your children to anger by the way you treat them…….

Ephesians 6:1 Children, obey your parents in the Lord, for this is right. [2] "Honour your father and mother"—which is the first commandment with a promise—[3] "so that it may go well with you and that you may enjoy long life on the earth.

From the above scriptures we can deduce that everyone has a part to play in order for a person's destiny to be discovered.

In a home where the parent create the right atmosphere and conducive environment for a healthy relationship with the young person, both parties can work together to discover the precious purpose.

Process to Purpose

Sometimes the process to a Purpose can be rough and rugged

- 11Then the angel of the LORD came and sat under the oak that was in Ophrah, which belonged to Joash the Abiezrite as his son *Gideon was beating out wheat in the wine press in order to save it from the Midianites.."...*

- 12The angel of the LORD appeared to him and said to him, "The LORD is with you, O valiant warrior." 13Then Gideon said to him, "O my lord, if the LORD is with us, why then has all this happened to us? And where are all His miracles which our fathers told us about, saying, 'Did not the LORD bring us up from Egypt?' But now the LORD has abandoned us and given us into the hand of Midian

Gideon Destroys Baal's Altar

READ FULL ACCOUNT OF GIDEON'S PURPOSE

Pathway to Discovering your Purpose sometimes may feel like going through rough narrow crooked path. Gideon was in a place of fear of Median, he was beating Wheat in the Wine press to save it from the Medians. While Gideon was not sure about situations of his life, unknown to him, he was at the brink of stepping into his individual Life PURPOSE to start living his purpose.

30

Gideon Was on his own, doing what he knew how to do, more like his career or profession.

<u>*There was a NATIONAL Dilemna*</u>:   *Israel [A Nation]did evil in God's eyes*

In Judges 6:   Verse 3: Israel was Oppressed by Median, Amalekites & sons of the East...

In Verse 11: Prior to Purpose Discovery: ...Gideon was busy beating Wheat in the Wine Press... He was very busy having a career...

Purpose Identification: In Verse 12:   "O valiant warrior."
God Reveals His Individual Purpose. (He is a Warrior)
In Verse 13:   He complains & questions God.

- In Verse: 14: it is clear Gideon did not have **Knowledge of Self:** The LORD looked at him and said, **"Go in this your strength** and **deliver** Israel from the hand of Median". (*Gideon is a Deliverer but did not know it*)
- In Verse 15: **Self Criticism:** *"my family is the least* in Manasseh, and I am *the youngest in my father's house".* (Gideon looked down on his family and himself).
- In Verse 17 – 23: Gideon Doubted God: He Instructed God: He Tested God: but he later got convinced it's God revealing his individual Purpose.
- After Discovering his Purpose by God's help, Gideon became even more afraid.
- In Verse 24:   ...Gideon built an altar there to the LORD and named it
  The LORD is <u>Peace</u> [there is PEACE of mind] in PURPOSE discovery
- In Verse 27: WISDOM and HELP to fulfill Purpose

Gideon fulfilled Purpose feeling afraid, however, he was in **Obedience** to God and he was fully aware of his **individual Purpose** at this point.

31

Note: *Discovery of **your Individual Life Purpose** does not guarantee a trouble-free life. At times you may feel fear, uncertainty may surround you, but with God's help, 'You Will Discover and Fulfill your Purpose' you will have peace in the midst of all situations. You will know the 'solution' that you are meant to be to mankind and you will be happy living a purposeful life till the end.*

Chapter **3**

Geography of Purpose

Your purpose, (your assignment) has geographical relevance to it. You are not called to every person that is why in some places you may not be respected, regarded, valued recognized or celebrated. It shows that such crowds are not for you.

Matthew 13: 57 – 58 *57And they took offense at Him. But Jesus said to them, "Only in his hometown and in his own household is a prophet without honour." 58 He did not do many miracles there, because of their unbelief. Where a person or people don't see you as a solution, you won't be respected, believed, honoured or celebrated. Don't be disappointed if that happens to you in some places.*

In the book of Acts 13:2-4: 2 While they were serving the Lord and fasting, the Holy Spirit said, "Set apart for Me Barnabas and Saul (Paul) for the work (Purpose) to which I have called them." 3 Then after fasting and praying, they laid their hands on them [in approval and dedication] and sent them away [on their first journey]. (The Geography of Purpose).

⁴ So then, being sent out by the Holy Spirit, they went down to Seleucia, and from there they sailed to Cyprus. You have to locate the geography of your purpose and deliver the solution God has made you to those at the location of your purpose. In

Matthew 15:24 *Then Jesus said to the woman, "I was sent only to help God's lost sheep--the people of Israel."*

- Where your individual life purpose is *'Discovered'* it may not be where it must be *'Fulfilled'*.
- The purpose may be discovered in obscurity but gets fulfilled on a mountain-top, deep valley, up in the air, at the sea, in a war zone or in a foreign venue or location that you or anyone else cannot imagine. Your purpose is a solution to a people somewhere.

Amazingly, when your life purpose is discovered it unveils fire that comes with it, that is why people who discover purpose are literally unstoppable. Wherever purpose is found no one can stop it.

Intermittent failures can't stop purpose. Criticism can't stop purpose. Limited resources can't stop purpose. Whenever purpose encounters obstacles, it uses it as a stepping stone to achieve fulfilment.

- David —As a boy he discovered purpose in the farm, looking after his father's sheep but, he fulfilled a purpose in a war zone and it climaxed at the Kings Palace as a King of Israel
- Samuel -As a young boy discovered purpose where he was serving under the supervision of Eli but, he fulfilled purpose nationwide across Israel.
- Joseph- As a little boy he got his purpose revealed to him in a dream in Israel, told his family but he was scorned, laugh at and despised. No one believed in him but, he fulfilled a purpose in an Egyptian prison and climaxed in his purpose at the rare Egyptian Pharaoh's Palace as the second in Command in a foreign land outside of his own native country.

- Mary Magdalene – was a town girl who was on the wrong side of life, not knowing a thing about her *individual life purpose* and drifted into obscurity. She was very disturbed, unstable and had lost her mind. *Read the book of Luke 8:2 and Mark 16:9* .....Jesus cleansed her of "seven demons".

  The Twelve were with Jesus, and also some women who had been cured of evil spirits and diseases: Mary from whom seven demons had come out—and many others.

At the right place at the right time, Mary encountered Gods love and she found herself on the path to discovering her individual life purpose. She met Jesus, she experienced love and realized she had a worth and value. She discovered purpose and lived to fulfill *her purpose,* today she is on record, in the number one most read book in the world 'The Bible' as one of the most notable women who ever lived.

As a young person, where you go to, who you spend your time with, how you live your life can affect your journey to discovering your purpose. Those friends or groups of people you associate with can affect you and your purpose.

- **Hadassah (*called Queen Esther*)**
  According to the Hebrew Bible, **Esther** was a Jewish queen of the Persian king Ahasuerus.

35

Queen Esther was a Jewish girl. The Jews had been driven out of Israel their homeland and were in exile in Persia (Babylon).

Although they did their best to make a living in this strange land, they prayed that someday they would be able to return to their home. Esther's uncle Mordechai, was the leader of the Jews.

Mordechai was Esther's uncle.
Before Esther became a Queen, when she was on the path to fulfill her unique *individual life purpose*

- She was living with her uncle

- She was not living at home with her parents

- She was in a foreign country

- They were in exile, driven out of their country

- At the time things did not seem to be going right at all.

Times were tough but, it was, in the middle of those challenging times that Esther got caught in the midst of a kings desire to marry a new wife who would be his queen. Esther was chosen and became the queen. Esther actually discovered her *Individual Purpose at the time when the Jews were facing a death threat in the land where Esther was Queen. After Modecia spoke to Esther about the situation on ground, possible death of all the Jews, Esther realised that she must speak to the King, (it was at that moment that she took to her purpose, by taking the risk of death to hopefully save the Jews.) Esther* lived to fulfill purpose and brought total freedom to her people in a foreign land.

Young Esther appeared as only peasant girl but when she realised that she was *destined* to save her people from death, she emerged as a deliverer whose Purpose was to save her people from death and destruction in a foreign country.

As a teenager or a young person, never let the negative situations in your life or your disadvantaged family background stop you from discovering your purpose.

You may be the next politician, a business person, a scientist or a medical professional who will deliver your people or nation. Don't let your present location and experiences inhibit your purpose discovery and fulfillment.

Acts of two Generations
Intriguing Story

There was a boy called Samuel - In 1 Samuel 3: 2 – 10: ² One night Eli (High Priest at Shiloh), whose eyes were becoming so weak that he could barely see, was lying down in his usual place. Samuel answered, "Here I am." ⁵ And he ran to Eli and said, "Here I am; you called me."

But Eli said, "I did not call; go back and lie down." So he went and lay down..

⁶ Again the Lᴏʀᴅ called, "Samuel!" And Samuel got up and went to Eli and said, "Here I am; you called me."

"My son," Eli said, "I did not call; go back and lie down."

⁷ *Now Samuel did not yet know the Lᴏʀᴅ: The word of the Lᴏʀᴅ had not yet been revealed to him.*

⁸ A third time the Lᴏʀᴅ called, "Samuel!" And Samuel got up and went to Eli and said, "Here I am; you called me."

Then Eli realized that the Lᴏʀᴅ was calling the boy. ⁹ So Eli told Samuel, "Go and lie down, and if he calls you, say,

'Speak, LORD, for your servant is listening.'" So Samuel went and lay down in his place.

10 The LORD came and stood there, calling as at the other times, "Samuel! Samuel!"

Then Samuel said, "Speak, for your servant is listening."

THE ART OF HEARING GOD

Just like Samuel under the supervision of Eli, as a young person, under your parent you can be helped if you position yourself to listen and obey.

As a young person, take it as a challenge that, if the young boy Samuel could hear God's voice, you too can hear God's voice. Yes! You can! Let your heart begin to want to hear God. The desire to hear God will get you to start hearing God. Yes, it's that simple. If you listen to your earthly Father you do hear him, similarly, if you listen to hear God's voice you will hear Him.

Every young person needs the guidance of parents or adults who can lead the way to purpose. Your parents are there for you, the guardian you have around you will help you, just open up and be obedient to them.

Parents ⟨–⟩ Children

Acts of Sons of Eli   1 Samuel 3: 11 – 13

Sons of Eli: [11] And the LORD said to Samuel: "See, I am about to do something in Israel that will make the ears of everyone who hears about it tingle. [12] At that time I will carry out against Eli everything I spoke against his family—from beginning to end.

[13] For I told him **(Eli)** that I would judge his family forever because of the sin, he knew about; his sons blasphemed God,[a]and he failed to restrain them.

Sons of Eli, representing teenagers/youth

From the above story, it is clear *that the younger generation* (sons of Eli), did not know their individual purpose and they could not discover it. **The older generation** (the Parent: Eli) did not guide them, correct them or show them the way to discover their individual purpose. They lived   carefree lifestyle, did lots of wrongs, made bad decisions that affected other people.   They used the name of God in vain *(blasphemy)*and caused lots of civil disturbances by way of antisocial behaviours. As a result of their actions, they never lived to discover their individual life purpose, God was angry with the parent for failing to be helpful to the children and as a result, both generations ended badly. *Read more of the example in 1 Samuel 3.*

To this end, both the *older generation* (parents/adults) and the younger generation (children/teenagers/<u>youth</u>) have a responsibility regarding the discovering of their individual life purpose. In order for you to discover your purpose and be the solution that you are meant to be to this world, you have to learn to be responsible and be teachable.

As a young person, you have a responsibility to listen to your parent or the adult to who you are accountable to. It is a parent who loves the child that will make the time to teach the young person. So, every young person needs to pay attention to parents and learn in total obedience. Teenagers, don't challenge your parent but, you can ask questions with reasonable interest, wanting to listen and understand what your parent's intention is for your best interest. Know that, for every decision your parent make, their intention is good, even when it does not make sense to you as a teenager or youth.

Chapter **4**

Understanding Youth Retention Strategy

How to Live Together and Stay Together As One Family

In my many years of working with teenagers and young adults, I have seen the disconnect that exists in families between teenagers and parents in the family circle. There is a huge gap in-between and it is worrying. We train both parents and the youth on the subject of youth retention, which means to have the young persons' mind stay within the family, in the family home. From talking with teenagers I have met a number of them who live in family homes but, they are not connected with their parents in the home. This is the case when there is no effective communication in the family, and it is not healthy if the family must live together and be happy together. Children and parents have their part to play in this matter of living together and staying together in the family.

As a teenager or a young adult, you may not like your parent's ideas, how they see life, how they give instructions or how they talk to you about things, but the first thing you must always remember is to try your best to always obey God first. *This is how you do that;* when He said in Ephesians 6: 1 − 2, that you should obey and honour your parents, He did not give conditions in which you should obey and honour them. *God did not say, obey and honour your parents 'if' they do certain things or make you feel good.* It's like saying, no matter how you feel about things, just obey and honour your parents or guardians without questioning their actions and picking on what you consider to be wrong in your parent's behaviour. You must not attach any conditions to obeying and honouring your parents, just do it always. Don't judge your parent's actions and then decide when to listen or when not to listen depending on how you feel about things. When you obey and honour your parents always, you attract blessings from God Himself. In your state of obedience to Gods word and to your parents, God himself will give you peace of mind to enjoy your family. If you live together with your parents, unity will have a place in your home for your sake, because you are in obedience to God and your parents.

This shows that for you as a young person to live and stay connected within your family, you have the responsibility to primarily obey and honour your parents or guardians, as you do that regularly you will have the blessing of God and peace upon your life, and you will live happily in your family home till you mature someday, you will depart from your family home to start your own life and family as an adult.

Young But Stressed and No One Seems To Notice

Teens and stress:
How to keep stress in check

According to the American Psychological Association – APA, Accessed 08/09/2018, *http://www.apa.org/helpcenter/stress-teens.aspx*. In 2013 a survey was conducted by the APA and the result shows that stress is common among teenagers. Teenagers who responded to the survey say that they are experiencing what they think are unhealthy levels of stress, especially during the school year. They report that school is the top source of stress for teenagers on account of issues such as getting into a good college of their desire or deciding what to do after high school.

The mind and body are intimately connected, and stress can affect the body *from head to toe.* The survey also found that teenagers experience emotional and physical symptoms of stress. Common symptoms include: feeling nervous or being anxious, tiredness, procrastinating or neglecting responsibilities, feeling overwhelmed, having negative thoughts and experiencing changes in sleeping habits. Problems with concentrating and changes in eating habits (eating too much or too little) all these are linked to stress.

Writing about the issue of stress among teenagers and young adults in this book is crucial and has to be considered in the process of walking toward discovering your purpose in life. For you, as a teenager or young adult to fight against stressful situations, experiences and overcome stress, there are a number of things you must know, understand and do.
First of all, teenagers and young adults need to know that parents, guardians or the older generations may not be sensitive to a teenager's stress point to a large degree. *When I was growing up, there was no awareness at all that young people can experience stress because they were generally considered as children or young enough not to have any worries in life.* Fortunately, that notion has

changed, research findings show that teenagers or young people, in general, can experience stress just as much as adults do with different issues of life challenges.

As a teenager or young person, once you feel stressed in any way, you should *understand* that it is **your responsibility** to inform your parent, guardian or any adult or authority that you are accountable to. Do not bottle stress inside of you or keep it from those who can listen to you and find ways to help. What **you must do is to talk about what is stressing you** and never assume they should know just because you live in the same house or chat all the time. Don't feel shame or withdrawn, everyone in one way or another do feel stressed with issues of life, but talking about it to someone who would listen, help or point you in the right direction is a good starting point to tackle stress and overcome it in your life. If you ever experience any of the above mentioned symptoms at the top of this page, at any point, you should immediately talk to your parent or guardian around who would listen to you, help or point you in the right direction for a solution. You can live a victorious life over stress as a teenager or young adult if you don't bottle it up or hide it from your parent or guardian.

Understanding Youth Retention Strategy

This is the kind of atmosphere desired in our families. If this is not happening yet in yours, then you can find ways, taking the simple advice and suggestions in this guide book, to start laying the foundation for it to start. Young people and parents can actually live together stay together as one blessed happy family. YES YOU CAN.

Live Together Stay Together As One Family

As a teenager or youth, staying connected with your family is necessary but, your parents can do little or nothing to help if you don't cooperate with them. It is, therefore, imperative that you find a way to settle down within the family home and be open to being actively part of the family where you belong. One effective way to start doing that is to stay focused, pay attention to parents and what is going on in the home so you can become aware and actively a part of the family in the home. Don't be absent-minded; don't walk away to support systems outside of the home. Make the decision to live together, stay together as one family that you are meant to be.

Here is a true life scenario to help you: *Emma is an American girl who got to understand that for her to discover and fulfill her purpose in life, she must work together with her parents. As a result, she started learning to pay more attention to things happening in the home. She started making suggestions about what she thinks could be done in situations, started telling her parents about things happening to her in her own world and learned to listen when her parents gave advice to her. Even at times when she thinks she has things figured out she would pray to seek God about her plans and still speaks to her parents to inform them about her thoughts. Through this process of open relationship with her parents, she went on to be successful in school and other areas of her life as she grew into an adult.*

Opening up to your parent(s) or guardian, not hiding things from them, will help you to build trust and develop a strong bond with them in the process of discovering your purpose in life. Remember that the primary role of parents or guardians is to guide you in the path of discovery and help you to achieve and fulfill it. Stay connected with your parents or guardian and stay connected with God.

In the home learn to open up and talk about issues, learn to chat more, learn to play and be happy in your own family home.

Loving even when it hurts

We train and encourage **teenagers** to learn to love Parents even when it hurts. Don't react to feelings, ask questions, and more questions until you release any tensions inside of you. Your questioning will help your parents to develop **Unrelenting Parenting skills and they will engage** and *help you.*

Teenagers and young people, in general, see things through the different lens of life, a lens –so different from that of parents and adults in general, different body language expressions, different ideas, and a different opinion about things. For there to be an active communication link, as a young person, you have to find a way to present yourself to your parents in a way that there can be an effective working communication link between you and your parents.

46

If you, being a teenager don't make the effort to create a communication link, there may not be a communication link with the older generation (your parent). Don't withdraw and recoil into yourself. Don't create a place for your parents to lose you without knowing it, *(Help your parents retain you in the family, keep your heart in the home).* There are a number of teenagers who are present in the house with their family but their minds are elsewhere. *(That is one reason why the young person would rather talk to their mate in school or to a stranger sometimes.)*   When there is a disconnect in the family between the young person and parents, it creates room for loneliness, depression, and fear in the mind. A disturbed and depressed state of mind can make the young person drift into thoughts of suicide (ideation) because they feel alone in this world even though they live in the same house with their parents and family.

Don't let your parents lose you. Communicate and express yourself freely to your parents at home. For the older generation to retain the younger generation there has to be trust. Your parents want to be able to build trust with you, so respect the instructions and house rules to learn in obedience. Learn to understand your parent and connect with them through the building of a relationship, and if you do, your parents will equally make an effort to learn of you, by learning to communicate and be more friendly. We advise families to stop blaming one another if things go wrong in the home, as human beings if a mistake happens, we need to correct one another in love and stay connected together. Home and family environment is the best place where teenagers and young people can feel the sense of safety, love, security, and confidence, so, help your parents create that safe environment for you at home by staying connected.

Loving even when it hurts

Live Together and Stay Together As One Family.

When love and unity become the norm and steady experience of the young person and parents alike, their mind will be at peace in the home and the atmosphere will be right as everyone will feel part of the family where they feel loved and cared for. Just as teenagers and young people need care from parents, parents also need the same from young people. It is a win-win situation.

In my years of working with teenagers and young people, when I listen to them and when they have the chance to speak about their attitude in the home, some would say that they drift away from their mind when they feel unloved, ignored, not corrected in love, and wrongly compared to their mates who are considered to be better than them. It is at that point of un-noticeable disconnect that parents lose teenagers, even though they live in the house their mind is elsewhere and sometimes their emotions get connected to someone or somewhere outside the home.

Fathers are called to make responsible fatherly contributions

Don't be that teenager or young person who loses interest in the family home. Losing interest in the home may be evident either by you physically leaving the home or being in the home and being absent minded. Both parties (Parents and Teenagers) need to work it out as a team in order to create the loving, happy family that everyone desire in the home. As a teenager or young person play your part, talk, ask questions, interact and respond.

in the upbringing of the teenagers and children in general. Fathers, defend the family, defend teenagers and build trust with them. It is understood that family situations differ, but whatever the family circumstances you face, do your best to keep your whole family together in love, this you must do conscientiously with perseverance.

Mothers are mostly known for comforting the whole family, bringing everyone around the dinner table. When there is a dispute, hurts, disagreements and quarrels and maybe fights in the home, mothers will always desire to comfort everyone.

As a teenager take your responsibility in the family:
As a teenager or a young person growing up, take responsibility for your actions and be accountable. That will make it easy for all the family to engage, discuss and come to an agreement on how to relate without prejudice in the family, learn to engage and sharing all things in common with love. When unity exists in the home, blessings will flow, it's true. (Read Psalm 133: 1 – 3 Behold, how good and how pleasant it is for brethren to **dwell together in unity!** ² It is like the precious ointment upon the head, that ran down upon the beard, even Aaron's beard: that went down to the skirts of his garments; ³ As the dew of Hermon, and as the dew that descended upon the mountains of Zion: **for there the** LORD **commanded the blessing**, even life for evermore).

Taking Responsibility in the home as a teenager or young person

In the family home, both parents and teenagers (children in general), have to work together to create a happy family atmosphere in the home.

We can be happy, laugh, tease one another and have fun in the home.

Note:

Every family has their daily living challenges. The families that appear to be happy and together are those families that when issues arise, they always find a place to talk about it, hear each others opinion, respect everyone's opinion and come to a common agreement over the issue on hand. With that kind of approach to family matters, a family can't go wrong. Teenagers, be advised to talk to parents, ask questions and be obedient as you walk through discovering your purpose in life under your parent's supervision.

Family

VISION OF PURPOSE

Taking Ownership of Youth development with – Vision of Purpose

How to see beyond your present situation to reach your purpose in life

In order for your parent or guardian to help you discover your purpose and help you work toward fulfilling it, you must decide to be committed to your parent. *(it has to be a heart-felt decision). This kind of commitment builds trust in the heart of the parent toward the younger generation.*
The adult has to see through the child to identify purpose and notice the solution that the purpose of the young person could be to this our world because, every young person has an imputed purpose hidden in them and must be discovered with dedicated help of the older generation. So open up to your parents and work together.

Two little sisters: Serena Williams and Venus Williams. Purpose discovered by help of the Parent and cooperation of the children. Then parent and children work together as a team to develop discovered purpose. 'But they had to cooperate with their parent for that to happen'.

Fulfilling Purpose, bringing hope and joy to people

Winners & Champions, *when they lose, they rise Up and come back to win, never giving up to Disappointments or intermittent failures.*(**Purpose Driven**)

In this life example the factors to consider include:

-**Vision of Purpose**

-**Time management**

-**Dedication**

-**Patience**

Cooperating With Your Parents For Your Good

The act of parents and adults taking ownership of youth development toward helping the youth discover their individual destiny in life epitomizes *'Love' for the child.* Parents/Guardians that succeed in helping their children to discover and fulfill their life Purpose are those parents who get **the cooperation of the young person**. Hence they can see through the child, see the purpose and decided to focus the child's inner strength on the path to achieve the purpose that has been discovered in the child's personality. Therefore, I hereby call teenagers and young adults alike to make life easy for your parents to help you. Cooperate with them always. The big secret to all of the achievements is respect and obey your parents without any conditions. Just obey always and you will reap the good rewards.

There are a lot of people who during their teenage and young adult life who have made a concerted effort to keep cooperating with their parents while they were growing up. One such good example is the first African American Present of USA. It may surprise you to know that Barack Obama during his childhood, teenage and young adult life was raise by a single mother. That goes to tell you that his family may not have been a perfect family but he cooperated with his single parent, discovered his purpose and lived to fulfil it. Your parent or guardian doesn't have to be perfect, all they need from you as a teenager or young adult is your cooperation and they will help you all the way to discover your purpose, work at it and help you live a fulfilled purposeful life.

A young Barack Obama as a Pirate with his mother Ann Dunham

Former US president "Barak Obama" is an example of fulfilling Purpose.	A Young Barack Obama, with his mother looking happy.
	Raised by Single parent (Mother), it could be said, mother saw *Purpose (a leader) in the child. With the Vision of* *Purpose, Time Management, Dedication & Patience.* *FIRST BLACK AMERICAN PRESIDENT (a Leader)* emerged. *Thanks to the parents and adults for support and help* *through the discovery Pathway to Purpose.*

Established relationship link in the home helps to work together, Parents are there to help teenagers and young people in general **"Discover their Purpose"** in life.

As a child, you have to believe that your parents will help in the revealed purpose when noticed or told. Adults, in general, are endowed with the great responsibility of helping the young person to discover the specific individual life purpose, but the process can be filled with some uncertainties, as human beings we can only see so far, but with the vision of purpose in mind, uncertainties can't stop the fire that drives the heart to discover *purpose*.

Don't get too busy with yourself and fail to be close to your parents and family, make them your number one support system. Focus with the vision of purpose and you will see the support they will offer and know that if you succeed, the family succeeds. Family will offer support in love to help in discovering the given individual life *purpose in you*, so that, purpose can be fulfilled. '*Your purpose is what makes the child a solution to this world*'. Every young person is an asset to the world in their own little way, not a liability as it seems to be sometimes. Make yourself a desirable personality in your life through your purpose.

Chapter **5**

Don't Impose Career!
Discover Purpose

Don't Impose a Career On a Child but Help Discover *'Purpose'*

From my experience of teaching, lecturing, training, mentoring and leading young people, I have seen that lots of young people are often told by their parent, what they should study in college or the career path they want them to do in life. I have seen a lot of this in the developed world and in the developing world alike. During "Pathway to Discovering your Purpose training" there is a section known as "anonymous questioning section", during this section of the training, teenagers often do say that their parent has told them what they want them to study or what they want them, to become such as Lawyer, Doctor, Engineer, etc. The young person takes to the parents request without arguing most of the time, whereas the young person truly has something else in mind but can't go against the parent's instruction. So, the young person, trying to please the parent forsakes what they really feel lead to do *(the Purpose)*. This puts the young person in a position where they find the parent imposing a choice or an interest over them.

Every teenager/young person should know this:<u>Your Purpose is like your Thumb Print in life.</u>

According to *scientificamerican.com*, *"friction ridge skin (FRS) covering the surfaces of their hands .....is unique and permanent-- **no two individuals** (including identical twins) have the exact same FRS arrangement....."* Therefore, as a teenager, it suffice for you to know that your purpose in life is like your 'Fingerprint' in this world. Prior to the introduction of digital identification, the most prevalent way of identifying an individual has been by fingerprint. All over the world, the fingerprint is known to be unique to the individual, in a similar way, your purpose is unique to you, there is no other human being on Earth who shares your exact *Purpose*. **Your discovered purpose presents you as a solution to this world's problems**. The world is waiting for you to manifest your purpose, so, discover your purpose, ask for direction and start working it out as soon as possible. You can't risk being other people, be your purpose!

As a teenager, if your parents ask you to study a particular course so that you can enter into a career path that is against what you feel you really should do in life, (*you would appear to be at a fork-junction* and confused), don't remain confused, you need to find a way to talk with your parent(s) to let them know how you feel and what you would like to do. If you do, they will listen and hear you out. If you don't speak, things will remain the same, so it is better to speak up than keep silent and just do what your parents impose on you. Your purpose cannot be imposed on you, it has to be discovered and followed through to fulfillment.

Help your parent(s) to "Parent you with your *'Purpose'* in Mind.
Talk to them.

As a teenager or young adult, If you know that what your parent or guardian is asking you to do is not what you feel you want to do, don't be confused, talk to your parent and have a discussion about it. They will listen to you.

During parenting with Purpose training workshop/seminar, parents are taught not to impose their career choice upon their children because it is not the right way to give their children a good life for their future. "The *purpose"* is not by imposition, it is a hidden treasure within and it has to be discovered with the help of the parent. We train parents not to tell the child to study medicine in the University just because they love doctors or because they want the child to be able to look after them when they are grey haired and growing old and frail. Parents, don't ask your daughter to study dental nursing because of family dental problems history! Parent(s), don't ask your son to join the military because you consider him to be so stubborn and difficult for you to manage, thereby thinking that in the military he will go through rigorous training that will calm him down and teach him some senses!

Note for teenagers/Young Adults:

As a teenager/young adult, if you are told what to study or the career path to take and it happens not to be what you want to do, then, talk to your parent or guardian for an understanding, maybe in the process of discussion, purpose will emerge and be discovered.

Talk, ask questions and start engaging with your parents more than ever before so that, a close communication link between you and your parents will give a leeway to discovering your individual purpose *'the reason for your existence.*

To protect yourself from future frustration, disappointment and failure, you must not allow yourself to be misled and stray away from purpose following the imposed desire of your parents. To be fulfilled in life in the long run, you need to discover your purpose and live by it.

When a parent does not impose an interest upon the young person, but helps to discover the purpose of the young person, a new spirit of friendship relationship is created for the rest of their lives in the family. The young person will trust the parent and will not hesitate to discuss personal matters in the future because the young person has the confidence that they can have a say in matters of their own interest

56

You don't choose *Purpose*, It is given to you

One of the most powerful tools you have as a human being is the power of choice. In the same way, adults make choices, young people make choices too, but teenagers and young people need to confide in their parents in making choices due to the need for supervision and guidance in decision making . As a young person do not jump at making decisions thinking you know it all, you have to involve your parents in decision making, no matter how little or how big the decision might be.

Around the world, people everywhere choose their career of interest. Most of the times career is chosen because of the reward or benefits that is associated with it. The act of choosing a career path has been the trend in professional life for a very long time. Most career choices are made with a degree of excitement based on the prospects, but after a while, if the job becomes monotonous or mundane, or if the challenges are overwhelming they lose the excitement. As a result, over time, the interest in the job is lost and they complain, seek to move jobs or change career path because they are fed up with it.

It should be clarified that your life **Purpose** is not what you chose to do every day, neither your employment, nor the hobby that you enjoy or tasks that you are assigned to do regularly. Your purpose is far from all of those. *At creation, the Creator inputs purpose into you because God has a specific reason for creating you into existence.*

There is a reason why you exist, your purpose is like a hidden treasure inside of you. It is like a precious gold that you must dig deep to discover.

Raw Gold

Raw or rough gold has lots of dirt sticking to it and leaves very little to be desirable at sight.

Just like the gold, at initial discovery, it may **appear rough**, rugged and surrounded by lots of dirt that have to be washed away so that the actual beauty can show up, and for the real worth to be evaluated correctly. If you ask gold diggers in the gold mines, they will tell you that the process of discovering gold is painstaking, challenging, and sometimes it presents a tremendously high risk but, they will also tell you that when the gold is discovered, it is always considered to be worth the risk. Similarly, for your individual purpose, you have to dig deep, search your heart, pray to God and listen to hear and see your God-given purpose inside of you. At the point of discovery it may appear like a little glimpse of light from a distance but, if you continue working at it, its full measure of value will be seen by all in due course. *Your purpose makes you a solution and the solution you present to the world is what evaluates your worth in life.*

Just as God deposited gold in earth for mankind to discover and make wealth, in the same way, your personal purpose is a gift from God which He deposited inside of you at creation. You simply have to discover it and life a fulfilled life by it.

You may not see the full appearance of your purpose just at once, but you can know the direction of your purpose as you walk through the different stages of your life to the right path. Take one day at a time and you will find your purpose materializing clearer and clearer.

A good example was Joseph. He had a dream that the Sun, Moon and eleven stars were bowing down to him, but the family did not believe in him. So, we can say he discovered his purpose at a very young age, but the journey to his purpose was not evident for a while. In the dream he saw others bow to and worship him but, because, he was hated in his family, the brothers wanted to murder him, and they ended up selling him away as a slave to Egyptian slave traders.

Joseph sold as a slave by his brothers to Egyptian slave traders.

The brothers lied to their father that he was devoured by a wild animal. While in Egypt, Joseph was a slave serving in an Egyptian master's house 'Potiphar. He was falsely accused by Potiphar's wife. He was then thrown into jail (Egyptian prison). At the prison, he interpreted dreams to other prisoners and they all came to pass. Then King Pharoah had a dream that his magicians could not interpret, Joseph was recommended to King Pharoah and he was called by him to interpret the dream Pharaoh had. After Joseph interpreted Pharaoh's dream, he was celebrated and appointed the highest ministerial position in the land of Egypt. His purpose was at its climax there. Looking at the journey to his purpose, you would agree that sometimes the process of discovering and materializing your purpose in life can be filled with uncertainties and unpredictability. So all you need to do at the start of your purpose journey is to discover it, and then follow the trail of the pathway. You will eventually climax at your purpose.

Your purpose is given to you by God, it is not a thing that you grow up to choose like choosing a career, and it is a treasurable deposit inside of you. Seek to discover your purpose and you will find your purpose within you by God's grace.

People who are on the path to purpose are those that you can't quench their spirit. If a person working out their individual purpose falls seven times, they rise up seven times. If they fail they recover and rise up to glory. It only just takes a little more time but they always rise up to their feet again and again. There is strength and determination of purpose, it never gives up to challenges. Proverbs 24:16 " for though the righteous fall seven times, they rise again... "

Those who stray from purpose are easy to identify and we have a lots of people in all walks of life among today's older generation and the younger generation. Imagine a person who has spent many years studying medicine and qualifies as a medical doctor who, just a few years into practice, they discovered this is not for them. They don't seem to be enjoying the job. People sometimes envy that person and wish they could be like them but the public doesn't have a clue that the individual they are envying is actually not happy on the job, not satisfied and lack an absolute sense of fulfillment. Although the job is well paid, money or other forms of gratification are not the essence of purpose. A sense of fulfillment is the essence of purpose.

The problem may be that the doctor strayed away from the purpose and until such a person discovers their individual life purpose, they will never be fulfilled. Such a person needs to come to a place of discovering purpose so that their life can be enriched with absolute peace of mind and a total sense of fulfillment.

This man works as a computer analyst with a good salary, but most times when he returns from work he is complaining to his wife, not happy, Not satisfied, not fulfilled, so fed up, doesn't know what to do.

Disgruntled medical professional. We all need to live life knowing and fulfilling the individual purpose in life.

The above professionals are not in their 40s yet, but they are already fed-up with their working life. In your life you have to do something that connects you to your purpose so you can be happy, peaceful and fulfilled. Get help, *discover your*

Being able to discover your purpose and being in a position to present your purpose as a solution to some of the world's problems, is tantamount to your total sense of fulfillment. Nothing else can replace your purpose in your life. Don't just chose a career, discover your purpose and live it.

Chapter **6**

How can a person who is already in a career path discover purpose?

The Lawyer

Don't remind me time is money. I am the lawyer here!

The Client at the Law office has a legal dispute

Most people who started out by choosing their career or who a career was imposed upon by parents instead of discovering their purpose may be in that position wondering what to do about their given 'Purpose' and how to get back to discovering it. *Look at this scenario*: A man spent most of his life studying and practicing law. So we have a lawyer by career. This lawyer has been successful at the look of things around him.   He has his law firm, married to a beautiful woman of his dreams, has children, owns a family home and has a lovely family car that takes them everywhere they go. His law firm has been successful for about seven years and it seems to be progressing with a few employees. This Lawyer, Steve, a 37-year-old, happened to learn of the *"Pathway to*

Discovering Individual's Life Purpose". In the process of the journey to discovering his Life Purpose, it resonated with Steve that he indeed has his Individual life purpose as a *(Car mechanic).* This is totally parallel to the law career which has been thriving for most of his life. Over the years Steve has handled many challenging and sometimes very emotionally depressing individual, family, and community legal cases and had some really good victories but the impacts affected him each time. Although he was making a good living out of legal practice he recalls that he has never really had a true feeling of absolute peace of mind or total fulfillment of all of his success. After sober reflection and in-depth soul searching, Steve discovered that during his teenage years, prior to university, he had some challenges in some subjects to do with studying mechanical engineering at the University and therefore reverted to taking to Law with his student friends at the time. Steve was initially a keen lover of cars. He was always intrigued by the wiring, connections and the overall mechanics of the automobile, he loved the revving sound of healthy brand new cars, especially sports cars and 4 X 4s.

At the pathway to discovering his life purpose, Steve without any shadow of doubt ascertained that by Purpose, he was a would-be Mechanic instead of a lawyer. This is quite an intriguing outcome of a man's life Purpose discovery journey. At this junction, Steve knew he was not experiencing the fulfillment that comes with peace of mind in his law career. In the moment of discovery, the question was how can Steve come into his Purpose? Should he abandon his thriving law practice just to start walking in his newly discovered Life Purpose?. How is he going to tell his wife and family that he, at the age of 37 suddenly he has come to a realization of his

Life Purpose? There are so many questions to ask looking at Steve's position with his discovered *Purpose.*

With some help from business consultations, Steve sought Wisdom to make a decision that would help him make a successful and smooth transition from his current career to his newly discovered purpose. He wanted to make sure his income, his marriage, his family, and lifestyle would not be affected by any uncertain risk that may be associated with this transition. And above all other factors, Steve wanted to engage in his purpose to afford him the much-desired sense of fulfillment in life and peace of mind that comes with a purpose.

The wise decision that paid off was that Steve continued with law practice, a career he was used to and has built over the years. He then applied to undertake mechanical training at weekends in a reputable well-established car garage. Steve recalls that for many years he had not many happy conversations while at work in his legal practice. He was making money though, and he appeared to be carrying his client's traumatic and depressive emotions during their cases and true happiness and joy was not evident in Steve's daily life. Not long after Steve started his mechanic training, he noticed that whenever he was at the garage learning how to fix cars, he was always feeling great freedom. He was interacting with his trainer, chatting with some customers and just learning and enjoying the training with a high sense of freedom and joy which he could not explain, but all he deduced from this was that he was in the right place doing the right thing "working out his purpose". In the process, Steve realised people liked him in the garage and he was grasping the teaching he was getting, soon enough, he started servicing his own family car, his friend's cars, and in about six months he could fix more challenging car problems. Steve really loved cars and wanted to fix them to keep the cars on the road.

In about 12 months Steve realized that he was having a laugh and a life as a Mechanical, (Steve is not going through a career change, he was doing well in a legal practice but was not fulfilled) He just discovered Purpose. When Steve realized he had discovered his life purpose, he decided to employ a sound and trustworthy lawyer to run the law firm while he focused on fulfilling his purpose. He was excellent, cheerful, friendly, helpful and just so free and very content with himself. His family could see he works amazingly and positively different. The outcome was that the law firm kept running, lifestyle was sustained, and Steve focused on his discovered purpose and continued to live experiencing fulfillment and total peace of mind in himself.

Through the process of purpose discovering Steve went through phases of challenges, decision making, questioning and seeking answers, contending with objection from people and close families, worries about uncertainties and so many other challenges. However, despite all the fears and concerns, Steve could not be stopped, he went for his discovered life purpose and in the end his family and his skeptics celebrated his fulfillment and success. If you persevere to focus on your discovered purpose you will be celebrated and you will be the solution you were created to be to those around you and in the world.

When is the right time to discover your purpose?

We held a session in a place where a nine-year-old girl was present, at the end of the session during question time the little girl asked if she was too young to discover her Purpose? I thought, what an intelligent question from a little girl of her age, and I said, the fact that she had such a mature question coming from her young self is enough to say that she was not too young at all. There are several accounts of young children who discovered purpose before their teenage years. Examples abound: at a very young age the boy Jesus was known to have discovered his purpose: *Luke 4: 17 - 21:* *[17] and the scroll of the prophet Isaiah were handed to him. Unrolling it, **he found** (he discovered) the place where it is written:*

[18] "The Spirit of the Lord is on me because he has anointed me to proclaim good news to the poor. He has sent me to proclaim freedom for the prisoners and recovery of sight for the blind, to set the oppressed free, [19] to proclaim the year of the Lord's favour.
[20] Then he rolled up the scroll, gave it back to the attendant and sat down. The eyes of everyone in the synagogue were fastened on him. [21] He began by saying to them, "Today this scripture is fulfilled in your hearing."

> ➤ The boy Joseph was very little when he had a dream about his **Purpose** revealed to him, but he may not have understood all of it at the time.
> ➤ Mary, Jesus' Mother was a young girl when her purpose was revealed to her at the visit of the Angel.
> ➤ Samuel, was only a little servant boy when he entered into his purpose and lived to fulfill it.
> ➤ David, a little shepherd boy was young when he started walking in his purpose in life.
> ➤ In similar manner, a closer attention to the story of Venus and Serena Williams show that their purpose was discover at a very early stage of their upbringing.

If you pick one of the above characters and take a closer look at the story that describes their personality you will see evidence of the steps they took to discover purpose. *They all took Risk.*

Where there is no **risk taken**	no **return** will be received
• If there is no **seed sown**	there will be no **harvest**
• If there is no **faith** expressed	there will be no **progress** achieved
• If there is no **pain** expressed	there will be no **gain**
• If there is no **Cross** carried	there will be no **Crown**
• If there is no **pressure** on life	there will be no **pleasure** in life
• If there is no **sowing** in life	there will be no **reaping** for life

It's time for teenagers and young people everywhere to know that God in his infinite Wisdom is highly interested in working with young people, the future generation and He wants them to bring about change for His glory and for the fulfillment of Purpose in their lives, for the good of all across the land.

Chapter **7**

Understanding Youthful Challenges and Struggles

Teenagers and young people in general, need to understand that parents and adults are coming to the understanding that, teenagers do face challenges and everyday struggles that are much more than those faced by the older generations when they were growing up. Examples such as rampant bullying in schools, universities and social grounds, work environment and sometimes in the home and neighbourhood. Social media and the internet pose serious risks to young people's emotional and mental health and safety risk like have never been seen before.

From my personal experience of working with young people in social settings, teenagers that present challenging and antisocial behaviour are mostly victims of poor up bringing and domestic issues from homes where the adults failed to take responsibility to help the younger generation find their footing in life and discover Purpose.

Now is the right time for the young people to understand that there is a reason each one of them exists. The youth has to come to truly understand that their individual purpose in life is a solution that the world is waiting for, (*the youth need to see themselves as a solution to the world they live in*).

Young people that discover purpose and use it in life would be solution to some problems we have in the world today. The reason behind your existence (your purpose) has to be discovered so that you can be helped to focus on your individual purpose, maximize your potential and live a fulfilled life.

No matter what the challenges you may be facing as a teenager or a young person in life, you are needed, your purpose in life is desirable and you need to be real with your parents and the adults around you so that you can be assisted to discover your special purpose in life.

As a young person, take the courage, talk to your parents because they are accountable and responsible for you. They want to help you through the challenges and struggles you face daily in the home, school or in the community. The only way parents or adults can understand the challenges and struggles you are facing is by establishing a good relationship based on good communication and friendliness, no blame, no name calling, no cursing or swearing, and no comparison.

Youthful challenge and struggles

As a teenager or a young person, you need to give your parents the chance to help in mentoring you, because your parents will see through your area of strength and focus on your strength to build and develop your capacity to fulfill a discovered purpose. Parents have
the responsibility to teach young people how to be a solution by using their purpose to transform the world around them.

There are occasions when young people may perceive their purpose before the parents do, *that is why it is very important for young people to have a* good relationship that would facilitate them in communicating the purposes they see in themselves to their parent(s) or the adult to whom they are accountable.
Recall the boy Jesus at about age 12. He was able to speak to the adults around him who saw that He had a Purpose and he appeared to have discovered the purpose when He was given the Book of Isaiah to read. He saw where it was written of Him about His purpose in life. Jesus quickly noticed that His purpose was to save mankind so, He builds spiritual and physical capacity to accomplish His discovered purpose which the whole world is benefiting from through all generations.

The little boy Joseph, (the dreamer boy) was able to communicate his purpose to his family when he discovered it, because he had an open communication with his parents and family. Even though most of his family did not agree with the bigness of his revealed purpose, his brothers tried to kill him so that he would not be able to fulfill his purpose, but, all the way, the tenacity of purpose kept him strong, until he actualized his purpose and saved two great nations, Egypt and nation of Israel.

Young David discovered his purpose very early as a young boy. In his teenage years his discovered purpose brought him to the limelight when he presented a greatly desired solution to the Israelite nation by defeating the mighty warrior of the Philistines, Goliath. David utilized purpose because an adult allowed him the opportunity and, encouraged him, King Saul gave David the chance to do his purpose, if Saul who was the adult in position at the time did not give David the chance, David would not have fulfilled purpose at the time and place that he did. Therefore, all teenagers and every young person needs to understand that your parents and adult authorities around you matter a lot in you fulfilling your purpose. Build a good relationship, respect your parents and older people and you will be helped until your purpose is fully accomplished in life.

Looking at the storyline between David and King Soul, it suffices to say that you never know who God can use to help you fulfill purpose in life, so, just as you respect and honour your parents at home, do same to those people who come your way in life.

At the accomplishment of your purpose, everyone who hears of your deeds and those that witness the working of your purpose will all celebrate your accomplishments.

High Expectations from parents and adults

Sometimes it seems parents expect that young people should do certain things under their parents supervision. Naturally, the parent has a high expectation of children. In some ways, the high expectation is a positive thing that can help the child grow up with confidence. Young people who lack confidence are shy and withdrawn from parent and adults; they would rather talk to their mates about things in school or the playground.

From my experience of working with young people, they ask a lot of questions which one would think they should be asking their parents at home. However, it does not happen due to lack of communication, no established relationship; no trust and fear of unpredictable reaction from parents should that they ask certain questions. Young people are in a world of their own and they struggle with issues that they face in schools, friendships, community, and personal developmental issues to do with growth and hormonal bodily change.

For the most part, parents don't necessarily teach children to tell lies, cheat, steal, etc. but they automatically can do that. The reason is that human nature naturally does those things even though it leads them into countless trouble in the home and out in the communities. *Refer: Proverbs 22:15 Foolishness is bound in the heart of a child, but the rod of correction shall drive it far from him. (Teenagers and children, in general, need the parents to help develop good character in them and help them discover Purpose).*

A number of parents may not be aware of the above truth from the Word of God.

In life things do happen. Young people, like adults do make mistakes and sometimes learn from those mistakes. Young people obviously need to be helped and pointed in the right direction. We encourage every young person to ask for help. Taking responsibility as a young person is what we advocate because it is the right way to develop, mature, become accountable, reliable and develop as responsible citizens.

We have testimonials from young people who have taken the initiative to start engaging their parents, and this facilitates a good relationship that works out to the benefit of the family. When young people engage with parents, it enables parents to function and fulfill Proverbs 22: 6 Train up a child in the way he should go, And when he is old he will not depart from it. All children need to allow the parents to do their parenting work. It is a parental responsibility to train up the child and help the child to discoverer their purpose in life and live to fulfill their purpose. A fulfilled purpose is always a solution to some problem so, help your parents train you as a young person so that you can grow up to be the solution that you were created to be to the world.

Cultivate a Good Attitude

> **A negative thinker sees a difficulty in every opportunity**
> **A Positive thinker sees an opportunity in every difficulty**

To Every teenager and youth, there is a saying that; you reap what you sow or (what goes around comes around). That means if you sow a good attitude, you will in return reap a good attitude from parents and other people around you. Respect and obey your parent and do the same to other people because what you give to others in life is what you are given back in life.

An example of a good attitude toward your parent is the doing of Ephesians 6: 1 – 3 Children, obey your parents in the Lord, for this is right. [2] "Honour your father and mother"— which is the first commandment with a promise—[3] "so that it may go well with you and that you may enjoy long life on the earth." **Pause for a moment (***critical thinking***)**; if the Creator says that obeying your parent will give you long life, *what about if you do not obey*? Do you think not obeying your parent will give you the *opposite* of long life? I leave that to you to think about!

Having a good attitude toward your parent will move the hands of God from Heaven to bless you with long life on earth so that you can live long enough to fulfill your purpose to the glory of God and for your own happiness.

Young people who show a good attitude to their parents do attract a reciprocal good attitude from their own parent because, in return to their good attitude their parents end up showing them *Ephesians 6:4, it says, Fathers (parent), do not provoke your children to anger; instead, bring them up in the discipline and instruction of the Lord.*

As the saying goes, you reap what you sow, so, young people, teenagers, show good attitude to your parent and enjoy good attitude from your parent and those around you, plus a blessing of long life from God.

If you show a good attitude, your parent will trust you, give you responsibility and they will naturally have more confidence in you and consider you to be trustworthy. It gives grounds for a close relationship based on good rapport between you and your parent.

Chapter **8**

Dealing with Emotions

Internal & External Emotions

During teenage years puberty sets in. It is a time of big change inside and outside the body. It helps to know about the major physical changes in puberty so that everyone will be aware and expect those changes for girls and boys when these changes happen. Puberty is the time when the child moves through a series of significant, natural and healthy changes. These physical, psychological and emotional changes *signal the young person is moving from childhood to adolescence.* Changes in puberty include physical growth and development inside and outside children's bodies, changes to children's sexual organs and as children become teenagers, their brains grow and change. These changes affect thinking and behaviour. Teenagers; be advised that when you notice these changes, your parents need to be your support but you have to have an understanding that these changes are inevitable. You can help your parents build a healthy relationship with you all throughout your teenage year's developmental experience. During these years you will notice some changes in your attitude to sleep, risk-taking, and in some other areas of your individual life. Be close to your parents and talk to them about your experiences so that they can give you the maximum emotional support you need. Keep your emotional experiences within your family as it will make you a responsible and respectable teenager.

When does puberty start?

According to raisingchildren.net.au, *"Puberty starts when changes in the brain cause sex hormones to start being released in girls' ovaries and boys' testes. This usually happens around 10-11 years for girls and around 11-13 years for boys. But it's normal for the start of puberty to range from 8-13 years in girls and 9-14 years in boys. Every child is different. There's no way of knowing exactly when you will start puberty. Early changes in the brain and hormone levels can't be seen from the outside, so don't assume your parents would know if you don't communicate with them"*. For parental help, you need to communicate. Puberty can be completed in about 18 months, or it can take up to five years. This range is also completely normal.

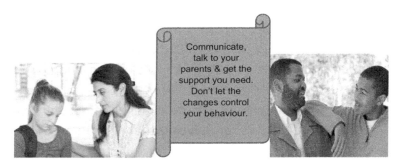

Communicate, talk to your parents & get the support you need. Don't let the changes control your behaviour.

Social Changes, Emotional Changes and Changes in Relationships

Adolescence is a time of big social changes, emotional changes and changes in relationships. These changes show that the teenager is forming an independent identity and learning to be an adult.

- Social changes in adolescence
- Emotional changes in adolescence
- Changes in relationships in adolescence

It is important to highlight that the various occurring changes in adolescence are more or less intertwined, if one is going wrong it affects the others.

Social changes in adolescence

Identity

Young people everywhere are busy, thinking and trying to discover who they are and where they fit in the world which has now turned into a small global village at the touch of a social media device. As a teenager you are no different, when you feel the pull you might notice you're trying out new clothing styles, music, art, friendship groups and so on. Friends, family, media, culture will help shape your choices in the years but you will need parental support so, talk to your parents all the time about these things.

Independence

In the process of maturity, you will probably want more independence about things like how you get to places, how you spend your time, whom you spend time with, what you spend money on and so on. As you become more independent, it'll probably mean some changes in your family routines and relationships, as well as your friendships. In all of these, you will need parental support, communicate and get close to your family for everything. There is no support system that compares to your parent and immediate family.

Responsibility

You might be keen to take on more responsibility both at home and at school. This could include things like cooking dinner once a week or being on the school council. Establish a sound and normal communication relationship with your family and get guidance and suggestions that will help you in becoming more responsible and reliable.

New Experiences

During this period you are likely to look for new experiences, including risky experiences. This is normal as you explore your own limits and abilities, as well as the boundary setting for yourself. You need to know that you are free to express yourself as an individual. But because of how a teenage brain develops, you might sometimes struggle with thinking through consequences and risks before you try something new. Remember you need parental guidance and support, therefore, communicate all the time. When trying out and exploring new experiences don't be intimated to share with your parents and ask for advice before you venture into trying it out. You parent might have been there, done that, so ask for your parental counsel, it will save you the mistakes they made in their time.

Social Changes, Emotional Changes and Changes In Relationships

Values

This is the time you start to develop a stronger individual set of values and morals. You'll instinctively question more things, and also learn that you are responsible for your own actions, decisions, and consequences. Your words and actions help shape your sense of 'right' and 'wrong'. Your values may reflect your family background. Your parent and responsible adults in your life can rightly influence your attitude in setting good values. The discipline from your parent as you grow up will reflect on your personal values in your future.

Influences

As a teenager, your friends and peers might influence you, particularly your behaviour, appearance, interests, sense of self and self-esteem. Give your parents the opportunity to have a big positive influence on long-term things like your career choices, values, and morals. The best way to get this right is to cooperate with your parents in discovering your purpose in life. When you do, you can focus on how to fulfill your Purpose in life and not allow others to influence you otherwise. Through my many year's experiences of working with teenagers, I discovered that lots of young people don't know their purpose in life, they are just copycats, so don't allow any of your peers to influence you, be who you are, walk in your purpose and be fulfilled in life. You are a solution to the world for your purpose.

Media

The power of the media is overwhelming, the internet, mobile phones, and social media can influence how you communicate with friends and learn about the world. As a young person lean more toward your family to learn about things organically rather than being overloaded with information from the social media that can't help you find your purpose in life. Don't allow the social media to dictate how you behave or do things. Connect with your family organically and be safe.

Emotional Changes

Sexual identity

As a teenager, through your physical development process, you might start having romantic feelings that might cause you to start wanting to enter into relationships or go on 'dates'. But these aren't always intimate relationships. For some young people, intimate or sexual relationships don't occur until later on in life. The wise thing you have to do is to feel free with your parents and let them know what is happening with you so that they can guide you through it all. Don't be shy to ask your mum or dad about these things. They can't know about it until you have told them. If you find yourself feeling like you are unsure about your sexuality, talk to your parents immediately as they are in good position to help you and lead you on the right path.

Moods and feelings
You might show strong feelings and intense emotions, and your moods might seem unpredictable. These emotional ups and downs can lead to increased conflict between you and your family but with this knowledge, you can be more aware to talk about how you feel to your parents. The moods and feelings happen partly because your brain is still learning how to control and express emotions in a grown-up way. Talk about how you feel to your parents and family; don't just act out your feelings.

Emotional changes in adolescence

Sensitivity to others
As you get older, you will get better at reading and understanding other people's emotions. But while you are developing these skills, it is possible to sometimes misread facial expressions or body language. Don't assume things about others, especially in the family. You should rather talk, ask questions and communicate with your parents who can help.

Self-consciousness
Teenage self-esteem is often affected by appearance – or by how teenagers think they look. As you develop, you might feel self-conscious about your physical appearance; you might also compare your body with those of your friends and peers. This is a part of the maturing process, however, as a young person, you need to talk to your parents and let them know what you are going through so that they can help and support you. The best self-conscious thing you can learn about yourself is to discover your individual purpose in life. Connect with your family and get the available help.

Relationship Changes

Decision-making

You might find yourself going through a stage where you seem to act without thinking a lot of the time. Your decision-making skills are still developing, and you are still learning that actions have consequences and even risks sometimes. Therefore, consult with your parents on every matter that requires your decision, matters such as choosing friends, where to go to, what to do about challenging issues in your personal life, how to react to peoples' behaviour, etc.

Changes in relationships in adolescence

One of the big changes you might notice is that you want to spend more time with friends and peers and less time with your parent and family. At that stage, you need to make a conscious effort to make friends with your parents and family and grow your internal communication within your family. This will help you to freely be able to discuss matters with your family and have a close family tie within your home. At the same time, it might seem like you and your family are having more arguments. This may be considered normal because as a young person, you are seeking more independence. It's also because you are starting to think more abstractly and to question different points of view. On top of this, you might upset people without meaning to, just because you don't always understand how your words and actions affect other people. It might help to know that **conflict tends to peak in early adolescence** and that these changes show that you are maturing. Even if you feel like you're arguing with your parents or sibling a lot now, it isn't likely to affect your relationship with your family in the long term if there is awareness about your personal developmental challenges. But it might be a good idea to develop some ways of managing conflict to help you through this stage in your relationship with your parents and family. According to raisingchildren.net.au *"Every child's social and emotional development is different. Your personal development is shaped by your own unique combination of genes, brain development, environment, experiences with family and friends, and community and culture"*.

Chapter 9

Building Self Confidence

There are different books on how to build self-confidence but, from the viewpoint of discovering 'Your Purpose in Life', our approach to building self-confidence will present a different insight that will focus on your discovered purpose.

Anybody can decide to approach the subject of building self-confidence in any way they choose. The armed robber builds up confidence thinking he is more powerful than everyone else because he has a gun in his hands. So he builds up his confidence on his gun. The corrupt banker builds up confidence saying to himself that he is so smart that his fraudulent scheme will elude everyone in the organisation, so he builds his confidence in his fraudulent plan. A man that is financially rich builds up his confidence in his accumulated financial wealth.

Your purpose in life is what will determine your fulfillment in life. Your purpose is what makes you different from everyone else. Your purpose makes you the solution that you were created to be in this world.

Your mind was given to you to serve you, not to master you. So, you have to master your mind and control your mind into doing what the Holy Spirit would lead you to do (Your Purpose).

Learning helps you build confidence, most successful people are mostly more learners than mentors... A mentor = a trusted teacher and a prodigy = a passionate learner. You can be one or both. If you are a passionate learner you need to ensure that you lean towards discovering your purpose in life so that you can focus your energy and passion into maximizing your potential in developing your purpose in life.

A renowned mentor once said he is 10% mentor and 90% prodigy, he learns more than he teaches.
Your mouth is meant to tell your mind what to do, so use your mouth to train your mind.
You have to find a hero as an example to follow – Paul said follow me as I follow Christ, Elisha followed Elijah, Naomi followed Ruth.

In the same way, as houses are built with a specific purpose in mind, so does God create every person with a specific purpose in mind. Every house is built with a purpose. Homeowners build houses to suit a purpose... hence you have homes with playgrounds, spacious kitchens to create room for dining, waterfalls to create a scene of movement, etc. You have to be willing to make some investment for your purpose, so, ask yourself, what investment are you willing to make for your mind? Investing in your mind will give you confidence like nothing else would. When your mind is educated about your purpose, nothing can stop you from achieving your God-given purpose in this life.

Discovered Purpose helps to build confidence

When you discover your purpose, you discover your confidence to set a S.M.A.R.T goal, *(a goal that is Specific, Measurable, Achievable, Realistic and time-bound)*. The goal has to be focused on your discovered purpose for life. Your mind needs pictures of where you want to go. Pictures give your mind the chance to talk to yourself. Such pictures brings you to a place of meditation, which means to mutter to your self. Meditate on God's word, meditate on the pictures of your desired destination which must be based on your discovered individual purpose in life.

Take Calculated Risks

As a teenager, risk-taking is non-avoidable, Don't be afraid to take the risk. Fear will steal your confidence and render you weak but, when you take the step to do something new with a picture to succeed, your self-confidence shoots up. Even when you feel fear, take the risk don't retreat. This kind of risk-taking is called 'calculated risk' Go for it.

Manage your weakness and strength

As a young person, learn to be comfortable with your weakness but, noticeable of your purpose in life. Your purpose will drive your passion to take a calculated risk. While you are encouraged to be comfortable with your weakness, you need to realize that you must focus your energy in developing your strength towards fulfilling your purpose in life. A number of young people I have worked with tend to spend most of their time working hard, trying to develop their weaknesses. That is not the right way to live life. If your focus on your strength and develop your strength, you will excel and nothing or no one can compare or compete with your strength. Discover your purpose in life, invest your strength into your purpose and be the best you can be at your purpose. Make your self a relevant solution to your world through your purpose.

Ask yourself, who do you give your service to? The only person between you and your future is the person you serve. The person you ought to serve is the person who has given you purpose and a future to live for. Knowing the person between you and your future will establish your confidence and this confidence will drive you to fulfill a purpose. Servanthood puts you in a position to build your confidence. Your purpose is what makes you the solution to the world around you. Discover your purpose, serve with your discovered purpose, be a solution to your world and you will be confident of who you are. Anything good should be earned and qualified. Your purpose is good, you have to discover it and qualify it through your servanthood.

Jesus displayed the greatest example of how to serve people with dignity; he stooped so low to the point of washing the feet of his disciples. The opportunity you get to serve others will turn your stepping stones to greatness. Learn to serve others with joy because your individual purpose was given to you to serve others by meeting their needs. You can only fulfill your purpose by serving or meeting needs.

In the book of Ruth 4:15: Boaz said and qualified Ruth you treat your mother-in-law better than seven sons. *And may he be to you a restorer of life and a nourisher of your old age; for your daughter-in-law, who loves you, who is better to you than seven sons, has borne him"*.

Law of Difference

As a young person with a desire to live and fulfil a purpose, there are a number of laws to enhance your confidence in life. One of the laws is the Law of Wisdom. Wisdom is the study of difference. *Pray that God gives you the wisdom to discover what makes you different from others.* Your difference is your value and worth. Also learn wisdom to know the difference in atmosphere, the difference in culture and so on. If you are sensitive to know the law of difference you will go far with your purpose in life. Many times people may call you names because you are different, don't be intimidated because if you stick to your difference (your Purpose) in a matter of time your critics will celebrate your fulfillment.

Decision
As you develop and mature, you will have to make hundreds of thousands of decisions in your life.   Your decision will decide the season of your life.   If you know your purpose then you can make relevant decisions that will facilitate your purpose's fulfillment. As a young person when making decisions you need to involve your parents and be honest with yourself.

Reaching
Your greatest fulfillment in life is reaching the climax of your purpose, knowing that every day of your life you are in your purpose meeting needs, and bringing joy to people's faces. Reaching that level in your purpose can only be the proof of passion stirred by your humility. Know your purpose and walking through the challenges of fulfilling all of it, you can't do it alone, take your parent and family along. Depending on your purpose, you may have professionals to help you in the process.
As a young person, you are required to participate in your purpose in life. In collaboration with your parents or guardians, you can climax in your purpose. You can live your whole life in error if you chose to show blindsight to your purpose. While you strive to fulfill a purpose in life, remember to cultivate the wisdom of God. The fear of God is the beginning of Wisdom. When you decide to start obeying your parents and honour them, you are obeying God and you are on track for long life and wisdom.

You are different
When you understand the law of difference, you will realize that your difference decides your importance; it decides who you pursue or follow in life. The problem you solve with your purpose determines your worth.   Your success is always priced through your difference.   The matter of discovering your purpose is of utmost importance. You must do inventory of your life to see what is in you that is not in others and thrive on your difference. Let

your parents and family help you show you how different you are to others within and outside the family.

Copy-Cat Suicide

As a teenager, even when you feel inadequate in yourself, or when you feel your mates are doing better than you at something, never make the mistake of taking steps to copy others. A lot of young people would rather copy other people, instead of discovering themselves and work out their individual purpose. Copycat suicide is when you decide to be another person that you were not created to be. Therefore, work at your own individual purpose, invest in your mind and discover what makes you different and offer your difference to the world and you will be celebrated because your purpose is a solution to the world around you. Communicate with your parents and family, and have a good relationship to make it easier for you.

Chapter **10**

Some Clues to Discovering Your Purpose

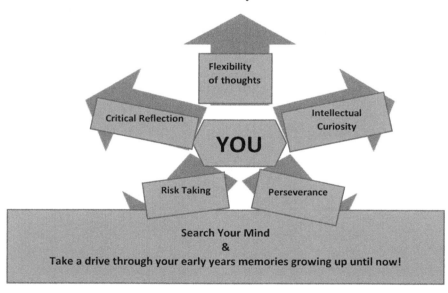

Some Purpose Indicators

Clue number 1:

What you hate is a clue is a clue to something that you are assigned to be a solution to!

- If you talk to lawyers who are fulfilling their purpose in legal practice, they will tell you they hated injustice. Some come from a family background where they suffered injustice and felt helpless and voiceless. So they just want to help others secure justice

- If you talk to men who have a passion to heal people, they will tell you they hated sickness & diseases. Some of them were sick to the point of death, hospitals gave up on them to die, but God healed them and gave them to the passion for healing the sick. For example, *According to healingandrevival.com, (....Oral Robert at age 16 had contracted tuberculosis. He returned home and eventually dropped to 120 pounds. He was a walking skeleton. God spoke to his older sister, Jewel, and told her that He was going to heal Oral. During this same time, Oral turned his heart back to God and gave his life to Christ. A traveling healing evangelist named George Moncey came to Ada and held meetings in a tent. Oral's elder brother was touched when he saw friends of his healed in the meeting. He decided that he should get Oral and bring him to be healed. On the way to the meeting God spoke to Oral and said "Son, I'm going to heal you and you are to take my healing power to your generation. You are to build me a University and build it on my authority and the Holy Spirit." Once at the meeting Oral waited until the very end. He was too sick to get up and receive prayer, and so had to wait for Moncey to come to him. At 11:00 at night his parents lifted him so he could stand. When Moncey prayed for him the power of God hit him and he was instantly healed. Not only that but every bit of his stutter was gone!)*

- Prosperity preachers have a passionate hatred for poverty and most of the time they will have come through the experience themselves.
- Farmers hate to see poor people not able to feed themselves, they hate to see their nation go through famine and starvation, so their passion to feed the nation drive them to farm and produce food and crops even though the farm business may not be paying them good wages or income. Some farmers are struggling financially but they are so happy to keep feeding the nation because they hate hunger and starvation.

Some Purpose Indicators.

- *If you hate drug addiction, that's a clue there is something that you can do about it while you are here.*

2. If Your Anger about something.

The word Anger has often been associated with doing wrong things because when people get angry about something they react negatively and cause damage(s) or destruction (s).

The important thing to know about ***Anger*** is that anger is a very good thing and it is more important than you think.

- According to madd.org, when a mother's child was killed by a drunk driver and she saw her child under the car dead, she got so angry and she started an Organisation called MADD – Mothers Against Drink Driving. She became a solution to her generation. She hated to see any more accidents. Something that makes you think about a solution that is not obvious to others, indicates your calling.

- When Moses saw a Hebrew slave beaten and oppressed by the Egyptian he got angry, that was a clue that he was a deliverer. He hated to see injustice and oppression done to people. It was after so many years that Moses as an adult had an encounter with God and discovered his purpose was to be a solution to the oppressed. He fulfilled his purpose when he turned against his adopted father King Pharaoh of Egypt and his adopted mother, daughter of Pharaoh of Egypt, and went on to deliver the oppressed Israelites from the oppressive government of the wicked King Pharaoh. Search your heart to see what makes you tick for action. Talk to your parent and get advice.

Anger is a clue to something that you are assigned to change while you are on the Earth. It is meant to serve as a pointer to your Purpose in Life. Don't waste your anger and don't misuse it. Anger is not meant to control you, you are meant to control your anger, to see through why you are angry about something and then think creatively to see a solution in your anger. Don't vent your anger on other people around you, it should be directed to resource a solution. An Irish doctor was not happy that poor people in Zambia were dying of minor sicknesses and diseases, so he went with his wife to Zambia and set up a medical care facility and it has grown into a large healthcare organisation where they treat people for free but he gets charitable support from around the world.

Anger is a **passion** requiring appropriate focus. Your anger is important because you can't conquer something you don't hate. It is very critical that you identify what burns as anger inside of you and then put that anger to creative use and a focus to change. You cannot make a concrete change without anger; anger is the birthplace of creativity. If you get this revelation you will see that your purpose carries along with it an intense passion stored up on your inside.

More about anger: A married man, (an IT professional) realised that he gets so angry that his wife does not tidy up the house as he would like it, he was always quarreling but nothing was changing, until he realised that it was no use fighting with his wife over it. He started supporting his wife to keep the house tidy to his taste, then, soon enough he discovered he had a purpose in hospitality and care. Your anger is not to fight others for what you want but to do for others what you are gifted to offer.

56

A well-managed anger will make you creative, perceptive and stir up discernment in you. Anger will make you hate the present to create the future you crave for. Your purpose is your life and it is your future. Talk to your parent about your purpose and work through it with their support.

Examine yourself

It is time for you to take the time to examine and scrutinize what

stirs anger in you. Look into your life and see what you don't like and what you would like to change or see differently. It is time for you to start questioning yourself, questioning yourself will lead to your discovering answers in due course. Generate a list of questions for yourself and you will see answers emerge forthwith. Emerging answers will connect to your Purpose. *Question opens the door to answers, the question leads to salvation.* In the Acts of the Apostles, Paul and Silas had been in prison, it was when the jailor started asking questions "what must I do to be saved?" that salvation came to the jailor. *Acts 16: 30 And he brought them out and said, "Sirs, what must I do to be saved?".* Your question will introduce you to the answer to your question. Your question will not go away until you arrive at an answer, the day you see a solution to your question, you will have laid hands on a purpose to work for life. The solution will usually bring peace, joy, and contentment, and a smile on your face.

Your question will get you to start examining yourself, to know what makes you different from others. Your purpose is what makes you distinct, and questioning will introduce you to your purpose. Young people are known for questioning a lot, use your questioning energy at discovering purpose.

I have met a number of people who have experienced God but, still don't know God's given purpose in their life; hence God has given birth to this ministry to bring this revelation to all generations. Ask God about your experience with Him and the Holy Spirit will reveal a purpose to you. *When you receive a revelation you will notice that your purpose is not far-fetched*

What grieves you is a clue to something you are assigned to heal. Look inside you to see: **what makes you cry, what** *makes you weep, and what gets your heart, what hurts you and what is the pain that you feel?* That is a clue to your assignment; your purpose is your assignment on planet earth.

Clue number 3: *What gets your heart could be your assignment (your 'Purpose')*

I once heard Dr. Mike Murdock say that he had a minister friend who had a heart for children who were poor and had no food to eat in Africa, up to 30,000 children in a local area. The minister's heart cry was to just feed the children but, in his ministry, they did not have the money to buy the food. When the minister spoke with Dr. Mike Murdock in his cry he said we have staff on the ground to feed these children, but we have no money to buy the food, and he said to Mike Murdock, if you buy the food we will feed them. Mike Murdock hearing this was moved with love for the children and his ministry provided the money for the food while his friend's ministry bought the food and fed the children. Mike Murdock does this monthly, thereby fulfilling the purpose of a financier and his minster friend fulfils the purpose of hospitality taking care of the children and looking after their wellbeing.

Fulfilling Purpose.

1. He gave the money.

3. They ate the food   2. They bought the food

and were happy.   and fed the children.

Your purpose is usually bigger than yourself, your purpose is not for your selfish consumption,   When you discover your personal purpose and begin to pursue fulfillment, you then become an open channel through whom God's blessings flow to other people in need.   When you are on Purpose, you attract blessings because your Purpose makes you a solution.   Therefore, when you are fulfilling your purpose you end up bringing a solution to peoples situations and all the people who benefit from the solution end up praying for you and blessing you.

4. **What makes you cry**

What is it that makes you cry, that annoys you that moves your heart, and makes you ask questions? This is a clue to what solution you can be in your life while you are here in this world. It is really important for you to examine your emotions because you won't feel everybody's emotion but yours.

YOUR PURPOSE *(Assignment)* MAGNIFIES THE PROBLEM

When you are in the right place at the right time your Purpose will magnify the problem, you will see what others can't see and you will hear what others can't hear. *When an evangelist speaks to unbelievers he sees hell, the problem and equally, he sees abundant love from God to the people and he sees them getting saved.*

When a Faith healer is ministering to people he sees the sick and sees them healed. Your Purpose will make you see problems and also make you identify a solution which you can become.

Purpose Reflections

One other unique way by which you may discover your purpose in life, could be by reflecting on your early years growing up, prior to teen years. At one of our recent purpose discovery seminar workshops, we dealt with the subject of memory and reflections. During the workshop, some participants testified that from growing up, prior to teenage years, they had some degree of childhood interest and attachment to certain things that they naturally fancied and it was some kind of interest they held different from others.

Some Purpose indicators

The interest, attachment, and love for such things grew up with them but due to being told what to do, where to go and not being allowed to speak their own mind or express their opinion, they gave up what was suggested to them by parents or by friends who had a strong influence over them. But now they are coming to the realisation that the childhood interest did not go away or die away, but it is still alive inside of them. Now, they seem to have realised there is an evidence of purpose but they have to now search their life, their soul and ascertain what purpose their life holds in inside of them. A final year student looking to enter into university realises the course the parent wanted him to do is not what he really thinks he should study. He grew up knowing he loved to fix mechanical equipment that is broken, he really wants to study engineering but his parents told him to study a different course. Now he is planning to have a chat with his parent with the clear understanding that he believes he has a purpose to live life and fix problems for people by fix things. As a young person once you have a clear knowledge about your purpose, talk to your parent and make a joint informed decision so that you can live life to fulfill your destiny and be satisfied.

When you discover your purpose you will be so fired up that nothing and no one can stop you! People in pursuit of purpose don't complain, they don't quit, they don't compete with others, and they focus and do the thing that they know to do. Young people who discover purpose revert all their energy into their discovered purpose, they stay out of trouble and they usually achieve their set goals in life.

Chapter **11**

Purpose Rebellion

If you rebel against your Purpose, What happens?

If you rebel against your purpose in life, God may permit some (painful) experiences to redirect you on the right path. You have to discover your purpose; don't be the last person to know your assignment. God so believes in your purpose that if He has to allow you go through painful experiences to correct you he may do so for your own good.

Jonah rebelled against his God-Given Purpose...

Jonah in Whale's belly

In the book of Jonah 1: 1-4

1 The word of the LORD came to Jonah .... 2 "Go to the great city of Nineveh and preach against it, because its wickedness has come up before me." 3 But Jonah ran away from the LORD ..... to Joppa, where he found a ship ......and sailed for Tarshish .4 Then the LORD sent a great wind .... a violent storm..

Discover your purpose, (your assignment), and just go for it. It's not worth the pain to rebel against what God has assigned as your purpose because, God will permit correction. You may not like some part of your assignment, but, you just have to do it and be fulfilled, so that God will take His glory in your fulfilled purpose in this life.

Setting Goal & Taking Risk

We train teenagers and adults in goals setting and taking calculated risks. People everywhere set goals without knowing where they are heading, and not being sure what to do. They do this in the fashion of trial and error, if it works they stay for some time while it's working, but if it fails they get disappointed and quit.

The best way to learn goal setting that works and risk-taking that pays off, is to ensure that your goal is S.M.A.R.T (your goal must be: Specific focusing on your purpose, you have to be sure that your outcome or result will be Measurable, ensure your goal is streamlined for achievement, that your goal is a realistic one, and that you can set time to achieve the goal). In order to set a S.M.A.R.T goal you need to, first of all, discover your purpose. Then focus all your strength and energy on your purpose, with such undistracted focus you will end up working at your purpose, and because you set your goal to have your purpose on focus, you would be taking a calculated risk knowing that, you are on course working at a solution that will meet a need in the world around you.

Setting Goal, Focusing on Purpose

When you set a goal that is focused on your discovered *purpose*, you can't go wrong, even if you fall or fail due to human error, you will always bounce back and stand up stronger than before. That is what you notice about people who are working on their purpose or their assignment in life. An example that may make simple sense is a man called Thomas Edison, Due to the numerous times he tried his electricity bulb invention that did not work, he was asked about the failures but, Edison replied, "I didn't fail **1,000 times.**

The light bulb was an invention with 1,000 steps." "Great success is built on failure, frustration, even catastrophe."

Why did Jesus not give up at the horrible and humiliating death at the cross? He did not give up because He knew He was on his purpose, so He fixed His focus on His purpose, seeing the glory that was laid up for Him.

Why did Joseph not give up at the Egyptian prison when he was falsely accused by his master's wife and jailed? Why did he not become a sadistic and nihilistic teenager and hate his brothers? Why didn't he get depressed about life during all the horrible tortures he experienced as a teenager growing up? He knew he was working towards his purpose, he knew that someday he was going to see the full manifestation of his purpose. People that know purpose are unstoppable; you can be one of them!

Parental Foresight

Teenagers and children, in general, are advised to pay attention to parental guidance. Parental roles in a child's upbringing are so important that it can not be taken for granted by anyone, Often times, parents train, mentor, coach, guide and lead the child into discovering their purpose. God has charged parents with the responsibilities to raise their children in the way that he should go so that when he grows up he will not depart from the way. Teenagers need to have an open communication with parents all through the process of finding their purpose to fulfill it. Talk to your parent about how you feel, what is going on in your head because your parent will provide the help and support that will last you a lifetime.

The Holy Spirit

In Johns 16:13 we are told: But when he, the Spirit of truth, comes, he will **guide** you into all the truth. He will not speak on his own; he will speak only what he hears, and he will tell you what is yet to come.

You need to understand that the Holy Spirit is the only one who can reveal your purpose and guide you on how to fulfill it through the various phases of your life. Keep your parents and the Holy Spirit as your closer best friends.

Receive the Holy Spirit

Why Teenagers and Young People Need Their Parent and The Holy Spirit to Discover Their Purpose!

In the business world, the factors below are responsible for the failures of small businesses. As a teenager or a young person, you need to understand that your Purpose is your business in life. Just as these factors contribute to the failures of small businesses, it can equally contribute to failure to achieving your purpose even after it is discovered. Therefore, it is crucial that you involve your parents in every aspect of your life and your purpose. Even if you were smart and intelligent enough to discover your purpose by yourself, you ought to stick with your parents to guide you through the process of actualising your purpose in life. Every teenager and young person has a long way to go to develop all these factors below hence parental guidance is highly advised. Form a good relationship with your parents and make them your best friend as you grow and develop physically, emotionally and mentally. The people in the world, who do business without the help of the Holy

Spirit, run a high risk of failing because they don't have the Holy Spirit in them and they can't hear Him.

From my many years of working with teenagers and young adults, I have seen and met a lot of young people who attend church because their parents bring them to church, but not of their own accord, they don't actually have a personal relationship with God, the Holy Spirit or Jesus. As a teenager or young person, you need to develop your own personal relationship with the Holy Spirit, through believing in Jesus Christ and accepting Him into your heart as your personal Lord and Saviour. Do this and mean it from your heart. If you want to live this life and fulfill your purpose, this is where you start from.

Furthermore, the Holy Spirit knows everything that you need to know, so make sure that you receive the Holy Spirit into your heart, pray to God and listen to hear the voice of the Holy Spirit when He is speaking to you and directing you, because He is the Only One that cannot make mistakes and cannot mislead you. Trust the Holy Spirit to reveal your Purpose to you and He will gladly do that if you stick with Him as you grow and develop in life.

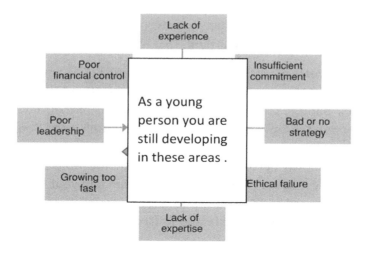

As a young person, you need your parents and the Holy Spirit.

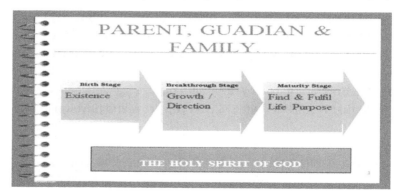

For you to have come into this world to exist through your parents and the Holy Spirit of God was involved. Through the whole process of your growing up till now, they have all been involved. For you to achieve the fulfillment of your purpose in life you need your parents or your guardian, you need your family and the Holy Spirit of God whom you received when you accept Jesus Christ into your life. You need to develop a close relationship with these so that you can walk through life to succeed and be fulfilled.

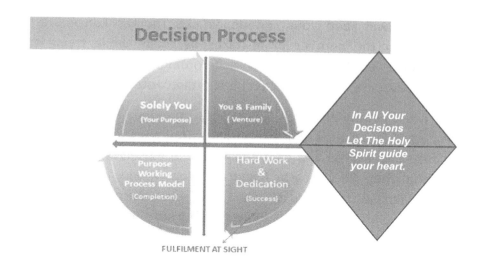

Decision Process

Solely You (Your Purpose)

You & Family (Venture)

Purpose Working Process Model (Completion)

Hard Work & Dedication (Success)

In All Your Decisions Let The Holy Spirit guide your heart.

FULFILMENT AT SIGHT

Knowing Your Self on Purpose

After discovering purpose, the idea of knowing your- self is about trying to recondition the way you think about yourself. Now, you have to start focusing on your discovered purpose. In building your self-confidence, know your strengths and weaknesses, but focus on developing your strength. Realise that in the process of life you will make mistakes but don't let the mistakes hunt you. When you accomplish things and people compliment you, make sure you accept complements sociably and do pat yourself on the back in those moments. During your learning process in life, whenever you get criticised, use it as a learning experience and try to always stay cheerful and have a positive and confident look on life. *Referenced at skillsyouneed.com*

The finest way to build self-confidence is to, first of all, discover your purpose, and then discover your strength within your purpose. People who discover their purpose, usually find their strength within the purpose, then harness their strength toward fulfilling the purpose. When you focus your strength on your purpose, you will naturally be confident, even if you make mistakes,...

..you will keep your confidence like Thomas Edison. No matter the number of mistakes he made while trying to invent electric bulbs, his self-confidence was unshaken because he was working on his self-discovered purpose.

Most people who don't have self-confidence are those that don't know their purpose in life. They end up focusing on their weakness and continually beat themselves over things that they did wrong or failed at. Stop working hard at your weakness, trying to fix it. Get help, train and develop yourself, discover your individual purpose in life and spend quality time investing your strength in building your purpose. When you invest in your purpose you will never lose, even if you fall seven times, you will rise up again seven times. Proverb 24:16

Discover your purpose, find your strength within your purpose and harness your strength in accomplishing your purpose so that, you can maximise your fulfillment in this life. Don't waste your time working on improving yourself on things you are not good at, instead focus your energy on your area of purpose that you love to live for.

Build Capacity

Once you are on your purpose, it becomes imperative that you build the maximum amount of capacity based on the knowledge you have of your purpose. Then you can work on the solution that you can produce for the benefit of everyone around you because your purpose is actually for the benefit of others while you experience the fulfillment. Every time you aim to double your capacity, you generate more solution to help those around you. You purpose makes you a solution to your world.

Maximising your Potentials

Your potentials lie within your but shows the things you are naturally good at. A person, who is a teacher on purpose, would teach and carry the heart of the learners along with him but, in order to maximize the potential, the person has to continuously train and develop self. Continually challenge your thinking, adopt a personal development mind-set, develop the attitude of a lifelong learner and build a winning team around yourself.

A fulfilled life of Purpose

A discovered purpose, backed up with a well-informed decision can eliminate failure, disappointment, stress, and fulfilment in life. Therefore, discover your purpose, follow it and be fulfilled in life with absolute peace of mind.

Pray
Dear Heavenly Father,

From my heart I thank you for creating me into existence with a purpose that you have deposited inside of me. I know that I need to accept Jesus into my heart and have a personal relationship with him as my Lord and Saviour for the forgiveness of my sins. Jesus, I ask you to come into my heart, forgive my sins and save my soul. I also ask you Holy Spirit of God, to come into my life and lead me to discover my purpose and also help me to walk through life and fulfil my God-given purpose so that I can be fulfilled in this life by using my purpose to provide a solution to this world in my own little way, to the glory of God, in Jesus name, Amen.

Reference

1   Collins Dictionary, Accessed 08/09/2018,
    https://www.collinsdictionary.com/dictionary/english/purpose

2   American Psychological Association – APA, Accessed
    08/09/2018, http://www.apa.org/helpcenter/stress-teens.aspx

3   *Purpose of Water: https://www.everydayhealth.com/water-health/water-body-health.aspx, Viewed 19/02/2018*

4   *Purpose of Trees: https://www.treepeople.org/tree-benefits. Viewed 19/2/2018*

5   *Children Development: https://www.webmd.com/children/tc/cognitive-development-ages-15-to-18-years-topic-overview, Viewed 27/1/2018*

6   Marys' question: Bible, Luke 1:34 "Seeing I am a virgin…. "

7   *Luke 8:2*

8   *Mark 16:9*

9   1 Samuel 3: 11 – 13

10 Ephesians 6: 1 – 2

11 *Psalm 133: 1 – 3*

12 *https://www.pinterest.ie/pin/457819118340542347/?lp=true Viewed 24/2/2018*

13 *https://www.scientificamerican.com/article/are-ones-fingerprints-sim/ viewed 16/3/2018*

14 *Luke 4: 17 – 21*

15 http://raisingchildren.net.au/articles/physical_changes_teenagers.html#What: viewed 28/2/2018

16 *http://raisingchildren.net.au/articles/social_and_emotional_development_teenagers.html; viewed 28/2/2018*

17 *https://www.skillsyouneed.com/ps/confidence.html . Viewed 2/4/2018*

18 *Ruth 4.15*

19 *http://healingandrevival.com/BioORoberts.htm viewed 4/6/2018*

20 https://www.madd.org/. viewed 12/3/2018

21 *Dr. Mike Murdock*

Gratitude

Thank you for taking the time to read this book, we pray that God through the Holy Spirit will help you to walk through life, discover and fulfil your purpose to the glory of God, to the happiness of the people you will provide a solution to, using your purpose and to the fullness of your joy and peace of mind knowing that you are living life and fulfilling your God-given purpose.

God loves you and that will never change.

Contact:

S.M.A.R.T GOAL TRAINING, IRELAND

For information about our training for the "Pathway to Purpose Discovery", you can visit our website and get in touch with us.

Email: admin@smartgoaltraining.com
www.facebook.com/SMARTGOALSTRAINING
https://twitter.com/smartgoal01
website: www.smartgoaltraining.com
Phone:+353 87 10 96 951

Made in the USA
Middletown, DE
14 July 2019